Signs of Grace

Signs of Grace

Sacraments in Poetry and Prose

DAVID BROWN
and
DAVID FULLER

MOREHOUSE PUBLISHING

Editorial material © David Brown and David Fuller 1995
See the Acknowledgements on pp. xi–xii for further copyright information on individual
items.

First published in the UK by Cassell

First American edition published by
Morehouse Publishing

Editorial Office
871 Ethan Allen Highway
Ridgefield, CT 06877

Corporate Office
P.O. Box 1321
Harrisburg, PA 17105

A catalog record for this book is available from the Library of Congress.

ISBN 0–8192–1654–2

Authors' photographs on cover by Ines Sanmiguel

Typeset by York House Typographic Ltd
Printed and bound in Great Britain by Mackays of Chatham plc.

CONTENTS

FOREWORD

The Christian religion inherits so rich and varied a tradition of literature, including those two magnificent works of literary and spiritual genius, the King James Bible and the Anglican Book of Common Prayer, that it is not surprising that anthologists have drawn on religious writing, both prose and verse, even for collections which are primarily secular. The instinct in man to worship, to praise, to seek for a reality he can call God and for a meaning to human existence, has always been a powerful inspiration for novelists and poets and meets a universal response. One does not expect to find the epic poems of Milton or the poetry of Donne, Vaughan or Herbert only in specifically Christian anthologies. Other collections in recent years have been exclusively Christian, or at least religious in the wider sense of the word. *Signs of Grace*, compiled by David Brown and David Fuller, is new in both conception and execution. Here a theologian and a lecturer in English Literature have co-operated to provide an anthology of poetry and prose based on the seven sacraments of Christianity and in doing so have produced a book which is as illuminating as it is richly satisfying.

When I attended my church school in Ludlow nearly seventy years ago, I was taught that a sacrament was the outward and visible sign of an inward and invisible grace, a definition obviously drawn from St Augustine. This fusion of the material – particularly bread, wine, oil and water – with the divine has been for me, and for millions, a powerful means of spiritual grace and refreshment. But I had not known until I read the Preface to *Signs of Grace* that Christianity had changed the number of its sacraments from the two – baptism and holy communion – instituted by Christ himself, to over thirty in the twelfth century, and then to the accepted seven. Now the word 'sacrament' is again used flexibly, the flexibility embraced by the two anthologists, who have organized their book in nine sections, the first dealing with the Creator's involvement with his creation, the natural world. Each section is prefaced by an explanatory note, a vital aid to understanding for those outside the Christian tradition and, for me, a fascinating insight into the compilers' interpretation of the nature of the sacrament and its relation to the chosen passages of prose and verse. It is only necessary to glance at the list of acknowledgements to see how widely David Brown and

David Fuller have ranged in their choice of material; *Signs of Grace*, like all good anthologies, provides the excitement of the new, the gratification of encountering the familiar and the occasional regret at the omission of an old favourite.

The compilers state in the Preface that, although particular passages or poems can be read in isolation, the book is designed to make continuous reading both possible and attractive. Undoubtedly this is an anthology which repays continuous reading, certainly by section, rather than the dipping-in which many collections invite by a deliberately less-organized and less thoughtful arrangement. Here the development of theme is important and the introductions to the sections are as fascinating as the illustrative passages chosen.

Not all the extracts are deeply serious, and not all the participants experience the spiritual grace for which they hope; even practising Christians have reservations about the theology of the sacramental life. There is disappointment, doubt, faith, frank disbelief, humour. Francis Kilvert tells how Mr Pope, the curate of Cusop, accompanying a farmer's daughter to her confirmation, was treated by the imperious Bishop of Hereford as a recalcitrant candidate and himself confirmed, to the great amusement of his parishioners. The eleven-year-old Nanda in Antonia White's *Frost in May* waits in vain for a spiritual revelation at her first communion, unable to pray or even to feel. The poet Geoffrey Hill writes of a communicant who accepts the validity of the Eucharist but remains emotionally dead, the heart's tough shell uncracked. Emma Bovary receives the last rites from the Abbé Bournisien but yet dies in horror and despair. Sacramental theology and the sacramental life offer no easy panacea for the ills of distracted humanity.

In their Preface the authors write that 'Not all those who are religious find a natural answering chord in religion's symbolic aspects. But for those who do the world is functioning sacramentally. Put at its simplest, this is to say that the symbols work.' Whether or not the symbols work for an individual reader, all those interested in the sacramental life and in the interaction of God with his creation will find in this anthology a rich source of enlightenment and pleasure.

© P.D. James

PREFACE

'Religions are poems', and 'God is the poetry caught in any religion'. So writes the Australian poet, Les Murray. Unlike, however, a poet like Matthew Arnold or a theologian such as Rudolph Bultmann, he intends no reduction of religion to either 'morality touched by emotion' or 'myth' requiring translation. Rather, the point is that both engage with symbols, and so say more than a literal utterance can convey. Not all those who are religious find a natural answering chord in religion's symbolic aspects. But for those who do the world is functioning sacramentally. Put at its simplest, this is to say that the symbols work. They no longer just point to something other than themselves: they also enable us to participate in it. In poetry the human imagination is engaged, often attempting to reach beyond the purely human. As Blake puts it, quoting St Paul, when we participate fully in a work of the imagination we 'rise from our graves' – ordinary untransformed awareness – 'to meet the Lord in the air' (1 Thess 4:17).

Art reaches towards the divine. The symbolic aspects of religion show the divine reaching towards us. The symbol is understood as having a divinely given transformative dimension: God as creator has put something of himself into it, and so it can both engage our imagination and work for our transformation. But what happens when the literary symbol and the religious are brought together? This anthology illustrates how the understanding of both can be mutually enriched.

Augustine defined a sacrament as 'the visible form of invisible grace'. Such mediation of the divine through the material most obviously occurs in the two sacraments generally accepted as instituted by Christ himself, baptism and eucharist. But where else? As late as the twelfth century as many as thirty were identified. Though the classic number came to be seven (some termed 'sacramental rites'), writers since the Second Vatican Council (1962–65) have once more extended the term – to speak, for instance, of Christ or the Church as sacrament – and this shows a flexibility which we follow here with our nine sections.

Though particular passages or poems can be read in isolation, this book is designed to make continuous reading both possible and attractive. Each section begins with an outline of its themes, while the order of the selections and their introductions attempt to highlight connections and pursue developing issues. With rare exceptions we have confined ourselves to British and American literature. In the case of early or difficult writing, the reader is helped by marginal glosses and by modernized spelling and punctuation.

A number of friends have read earlier versions of the manuscript in whole or in part; so we wish to record here our special thanks to Ann Loades, Stephen Pedley, Tom Craik, John McKinnell, Jean and Owen Rees, Ella Wright, Cynthia Fuller and David Gardner. We are also grateful to the following for various kinds of help and suggestions: Richard Bauckham, Nicholas Baumfield, Ronald Coppin, Robin Dix, Gregor Duncan, Michael Ferber, Michael Fraser, Sheridan Gilley, John Greaves, Gerard Hanratty, Susan and Evan Hughes, Ben Knights, Margaret Masson, Michael O'Neill, Amanda Piesse, John Polkinghorne, Gareth Reeves, Michael Schepers and Derek Todd.

ACKNOWLEDGEMENTS

Every effort has been made to locate copyright holders, though in a small number of cases this has proved impossible. We are grateful for permission to reprint the following copyright material:

W. H. Auden: Faber & Faber for a poem from *Thanksgiving for a Habitat* from *Collected Poems*, edited by E. Mendelson;

John Betjeman: John Murray for extract from *Summoned by Bells*;

Elizabeth Bishop: Farrar, Straus and Giroux, Inc. for 'Seascape' from *The Complete Poems, 1927–79*. Copyright 1979, 1983 by Alice Helen Methfessel;

Willa Cather: Virago for an extract from *O Pioneers!*;

Dick Davis: Anvil Press Poetry for 'Memories of Cochin' from *Seeing the World* (1980);

Carol Ann Duffy: Anvil Press Poetry for 'Confession' from *Mean Time* (1993);

T. S. Eliot: Faber & Faber for extract from *Four Quartets* from *Collected Poems 1909–62*;

David Gascoyne: Oxford University Press for 'Mozart: Sursum Corda' from *Collected Poems* (1988);

Graham Greene: Heinemann for extract from *Brighton Rock*;

Seamus Heaney: Faber & Faber for extract from *Station Island*;

Geoffrey Hill: Penguin Books Ltd for 'The Bidden Guest' from *For the Unfallen*;

P. D. James: Faber & Faber for extract from *The Children of Men*;

Elizabeth Jennings: Carcanet Press for 'Harvest and Consecration' and 'Visit to an Artist' from *Song for a Birth or a Death* and 'Thunder and a Boy' from *Growing Points*;

Denise Levertov: Bloodaxe Books Ltd, New Directions Publishing Corporation and Laurence Pollinger Ltd for 'Sunday Morning' from *With Eyes at the Back of Our Heads*;

Norman Lewis: Penguin Books Ltd for extract from *Jackdaw Cake*;

Derek Mahon: Oxford University Press for 'A Garage in Co. Cork' from *The Hunt by Night* (1982);

John Masefield: The Society of Authors as the literary representative of the

Estate of John Masefield for extract from *The Everlasting Mercy*;

Flannery O'Connor: Faber & Faber for two extracts from *The Complete Stories of Flannery O'Connor*;

Michael O'Neill: HarperCollins*Publishers* Ltd for 'Wedding Dress' from *The Stripped Bed*;

Kathleen Raine: Golgonooza Press for 'Word Made Flesh' from *The Pythoness*;

Anne Ridler: Carcanet Press for 'Cranmer and the Bread of Heaven' from *A Matter of Life and Death*;

Wallace Stevens: Faber & Faber for 'The American Sublime' from *Collected Poems*;

Dylan Thomas: J. M. Dent & Sons Ltd for 'This Bread I Break' from *The Poems*;

R. S. Thomas: Bloodaxe Books Ltd for a poem from 'Bleak Liturgies' from *Mass for Hard Times* (1992);

R. S. Thomas: J. M. Dent & Sons Ltd for 'The Country Clergy' from *Collected Poems 1945–90*;

Michel Tournier: HarperCollins*Publishers* Ltd for extract from *The Four Wise Men*;

Evelyn Waugh: Peters Fraser & Dunlop Group Ltd for extract from *Brideshead Revisited*;

Antonia White: Virago for extract from *Frost in May*.

A SACRAMENTAL WORLD

Introduction

Christian history inherited from Judaism a deep suspicion of any attempt to assign too exalted a role to nature. The people of Israel were surrounded by nature cults which reflected the rhythms of the agricultural year and which proved seductively attractive (cf. e.g. Hosea 2:1–20; Jer 19:1–6; Ezek 8:5–18), and it was only with difficulty that they were kept loyal to their covenant with God. From that struggle arose a sharp insistence upon the doctrine of *creatio ex nihilo*, the idea that God created the world from nothing and that therefore God and the world are two completely distinct entities. Such a view also stood in marked contrast to the two leading philosophies of the Roman world within which the initial Christian mission operated – Stoicism with its doctrine of complete divine immanence, and Platonism with its notion of emanation, that the world is a lesser level of divine reality which has 'flowed out' of God.

Conceptions similar to those of ancient philosophy continue to find a place today, particularly within Hinduism. Some versions of Christianity, by contrast, remain as insistent as ever upon the otherness of God. The sacramental tradition, however, takes a different view; it offers a way of linking world and God more closely, without compromising God's essential otherness. Indeed, the claim would be that such a link must be found; otherwise, God's role as creator is diminished. Any form of creativity involves putting something of oneself into the work, and in God's case this must surely involve creation reflecting his goodness, rationality and generosity.

A recurring image used in what follows to express this idea is the notion of nature as a second Bible, so intimately does it reflect the Creator's involvement. Nature is God's 'scriptures' (Clare) or 'lectures' (Vaughan) or even, paralleling the incarnation, 'Word made Flesh' (Raine). But, if that is so, why is that not always seen? Traherne and Jennings point to a lost childhood innocence; Hopkins blames the modern absence of intimate contact with nature; while Bishop and Blake both identify perversions of Christianity as the true cause. Yet for others direct experience of the divine presence in nature overwhelms other considerations. For Marvell and

Wordsworth God is at his closest in the natural world, and to this even the agnostic Shelley adds his assent. Perhaps that is why the image of nature also offering its praise to the Creator is such a prominent poetic theme – whether it be the trees of the forest as in Longfellow, flowers and birds as in Smart, or the gentle play of spring light as in Dickinson.

God's second book

John Clare was an agricultural labourer who for a time benefited from a fashion for rural poetry, of the kind also found in Burns. But much of his later life was spent in a mental asylum (here, 'in prison'). His poetry powerfully evokes the landscape of his native Northamptonshire. In this sonnet he uses an image at least as old as Augustine, of nature as God's second 'book' (after the Bible). Her flowers are heaven's 'very scriptures upon earth'; her works are without any of the 'leaven' of false religion (cf. Matt 16:11).

> Poets love nature, and themselves are love;
> The scorn of fools and mock of idle pride.
> The vile in nature worthless deeds approve:
> They court the vile, and spurn all good beside.
> Poets love nature like the calm of heaven;
> Her gifts like heaven's love spread far and wide.
> In all her works there are no signs of leaven;
> Sorrow abashes from her simple pride.   *retreats in embarrassment*
> Her flowers like pleasures have their season's birth
> And bloom through regions here below;
> They are her very scriptures upon earth,
> And teach us simple mirth where e'er we go.
> Even in prison they can solace me,
> For where they bloom God is, and I am free.
>
> John Clare (1793–1864).

Pointers to heaven

Henry Vaughan first endorses Clare's theme: the world contains 'lectures' for our eye and ear. But he then develops it in a specific way: wherever we turn we see nature striving upwards, and so giving a heavenly, less material message. Water turns to mist; earthy roots to flowers that blow in the wind; only human beings, like Issachar (Gen 49:14–15), are content to be weighed down and pulled towards earth. All nature is instructive, but, if we are blind to this, nature's extremes – tempest and drought – work on us like a steel on flint.

How is man parcelled out! how every hour
    Shows him himself, or something he should see!
    This late, long heat may his instruction be,
And tempests have more in them than a shower.

> *When nature on her bosom saw*
>   *Her infants die,*
> *And all her flowers withered to straw,*
>   *Her breasts grown dry;*
> *She made the earth, their nurse and tomb,*
>   *Sigh to the sky,*
> *'Til to those sighs fetched from her womb*
>   *Rain did reply.*
> *So in the midst of all her fears*
>   *And faint requests*
> *Her earnest sighs procured her tears*
>   *And filled her breasts.*

O that man could do so! that he would hear
    The world read to him! all the vast expense
    In the Creation shed, and slaved to sense,
Makes up but lectures for his eye and ear.

Sure, mighty love foreseeing the descent
    Of this poor creature, by a gracious art
    Hid in these low things snares to gain his heart,
And laid surprises in each element.

All things here show him heaven; *waters* that fall
    Chide and fly up; *mists* of corruptest foam
    Quit their first beds and mount; trees, herbs, flowers, all
Strive upwards still, and point him the way home.

How do they cast off grossness! Only *earth*,
    And *man* (like *Issachar*) in loads delight:
    Water's refined to *motion*, air to *light*,
Fire to all three, but man hath no such mirth.

Plants in the *root* with earth do most comply,
    Their *leaves* with water and humidity,
    The *flowers* to air draw near, and subtlety,
And *seeds* a kindred fire have with the sky.

All have their *keys*, and set *ascents*; but man,
    Though he knows these, and hath more of his own,
    Sleeps at the ladder's foot; alas! what can
These new discoveries do, except they drown?

Thus grovelling in the shade and darkness, he
    Sinks to a dead oblivion; and though all
    He sees (like *pyramids*) shoot from this ball,
And lessening still grow up invisibly,

Yet hugs he still his dirt: the *stuff* he wears
    And painted trimming takes down both his eyes;
    Heaven hath less beauty than the dust he spies,
And money better music than the *spheres*.

Life's but a blast, he knows it; what? shall straw,
    And bulrush-fetters temper his short hour?
    Must he nor sip, nor sing? grows ne'er a flower
To crown his temples? shall dreams be his law?

O foolish man! how hast thou lost thy sight?
    How is it that the sun to thee alone
    Is grown thick darkness, and thy bread a stone?
Hath flesh no softness now? midday no light?

Lord, thou didst put a soul here; if I must
    Be broke again, for flints will give no fire
    Without a steel, O let thy power clear
Thy gift once more, and grind this flint to dust!

                Henry Vaughan (1621–95), 'The Tempest'.

The grammar of the world

Vaughan was very interested in the *Hermetica*, third-century Gnostic texts associated with the name of Hermes Trismegistus and influential on the Platonism both of that time and of the seventeenth century. Kathleen Raine is a poet who has similar interests, in part because of her special concern with Blake and his unique adaptation of such ideas. While some versions of Platonism and Gnosticism are hostile to the world, this is not always the case. Vaughan exhibits a thoroughly sacramental attitude, while the title Kathleen Raine chose to give this poem ('Word Made Flesh') already indicates such an interest. The divine Word has taken flesh not only in the incarnation (John 1:14), but in the order and beauty of the world which we see everywhere about us. Only in the last line does another characteristic Platonic stress emerge, with talk of 'a spirit clothed in world': the higher spirit still remains essentially distinct from the matter within which it is embodied.

Word whose breath is the world-circling atmosphere,
Word that utters the world that turns the wind,
Word that articulates the bird that speeds upon the air,

Word that blazes out the trumpet of the sun,
Whose silence is the violin-music of the stars,
Whose melody is the dawn, and harmony the night,

Word traced in water of lakes, and light on water,
Light on still water, moving water, waterfall
And water colours of cloud, of dew, of spectral rain,

Word inscribed on stone, mountain range upon range of
      stone,
Word that is fire of the sun and fire within
Order of atoms, crystalline symmetry,

Grammar of five-fold rose and six-fold lily,
Spiral of leaves on a bough, helix of shells,
Rotation of twining plants on axes of darkness and light,

Instinctive wisdom of fish and lion and ram,
Rhythm of generation in flagellate and fern,
Flash of fin, beat of wing, heartbeat, beat of the dance,

Hieroglyph in whose exact precision is defined
Feather and insect-wing, refraction of multiple eyes,
Eyes of the creatures, oh myriadfold vision of the world,

Statement of mystery, how shall we name
A spirit clothed in world, a world made man?
    Kathleen Raine (b. 1908), 'Word Made Flesh' from *The Pythoness*.

Nature smudged

But if nature is a book there to be read, why do not all human beings perceive God in it? This was a question of concern to Hopkins, as a Jesuit priest. On the positive side, he stresses the concentration of the divine within nature; it flames and oozes out. Nonetheless, our vision is blurred by 'trade' – by which, Hopkins explains, he means all forms of human commerce and industry which either damage nature or prevent direct contact with it ('foot ... shod'). Even so, nature is inexhaustibly prolific, with the Spirit hovering creatively over the world (Gen 1:2).

The world is charged with the grandeur of God.
    It will flame out, like shining from shook foil;
    It gathers to a greatness, like the ooze of oil
Crushed. Why do men then now not reck his rod?
Generations have trod, have trod, have trod;
    And all is seared with trade; bleared, smeared, with toil;
    And wears man's smudge and shares man's smell: the soil

Is bare now, nor can foot feel, being shod.
And, for all this, nature is never spent;
    There lives the dearest freshness deep down things;
And though the last lights off the black West went,
    Oh, morning, at the brown brink eastward, springs –
Because the Holy Ghost over the bent
    World broods with warm breast and with ah! bright wings.

Gerard Manley Hopkins (1844–89), 'God's Grandeur'.

The Eden of childhood

Traherne, whose work was discovered in manuscript form only at the end of
the nineteenth century, was rector of Credenhill in Herefordshire, where he
had a number of mystical experiences. In this extract he describes his
innocent childhood vision of the world's miraculous beauty, and, like
Hopkins, ponders why we fail to see the Eden all around us. His explanation
is that childhood innocence is lost and we 'learn the dirty devices of this
world', which we must unlearn if the vision is to be restored. Then we will
discover 'something infinite behind everything'. 'Infinite' is one of Traherne's favourite words for God, and represents his attempt to harness
current ideas about the vastness of space to a positive theological purpose.

> Will you see the infancy of this sublime and celestial greatness?
> Those pure and virgin apprehensions I had from the womb, and
> that divine light wherewith I was born, are the best unto this day
> wherein I can see the universe. By the gift of God they attended
> me into the world, and by His special favour I remember them
> till now. Verily they seem the greatest gifts His wisdom could
> bestow, for without them all other gifts had been dead and vain.
> They are unattainable by book, and therefore I will teach them
> by experience. Pray for them earnestly: for they will make you
> angelical, and wholly celestial. Certainly Adam in Paradise had
> not more sweet and curious apprehensions of the world, than I
> when I was a child. . . .
>
> The corn was orient and immortal wheat, which never should be
> reaped, nor was ever sown. I thought it had stood from ever-
> lasting to everlasting. The dust and stones of the street were as
> precious as gold. The gates were at first the end of the world.
> The green trees when I saw them first through one of the gates
> transported and ravished me; their sweetness and unusual
> beauty made my heart to leap, and almost mad with ecstasy, they
> were such strange and wonderful things. The men! O what

venerable and reverend creatures did the aged seem! Immortal
cherubims! And young men glittering and sparkling angels, and
maids strange seraphic pieces of life and beauty! Boys and girls
tumbling in the street, and playing, were moving jewels. I knew
not that they were born or should die. But all things abided
eternally, as they were in their proper places. Eternity was
manifest in the light of the day, and something infinite behind
everything appeared, which talked with my expectation and
moved my desire. The city seemed to stand in Eden, or to be
built in Heaven. The streets were mine, the temple was mine,
the people were mine, their clothes and gold and silver was
mine, as much as their sparkling eyes, fair skins, and ruddy
faces. The skies were mine, and so were the sun and moon and
stars, and all the world was mine, and I the only spectator and
enjoyer of it. I knew no churlish proprieties, nor bounds, nor
divisions; but all proprieties and divisions were mine: all treasures and the possessors of them. So that with much ado I was
corrupted; and made to learn the dirty devices of this world.
Which now I unlearn, and become as it were a little child again,
that I may enter into the Kingdom of God.

> Thomas Traherne (1637–74), from 'The Third Century' from
> *Centuries of Meditations*.

The clerical lighthouse

Elizabeth Bishop is an American poet who was brought up in Nova Scotia.
This poem, which may go back to those roots, is in two parts. The first
paints the positive side of the scene in allusively religious terms – 'immaculate reflections', 'Gothic arches', 'tapestry for a Pope'; it all suggests
'heaven'. But the second half conjures up a different image: the clerically
dressed lighthouse detects threats of hell in the water and uses its foghorn
to blare out a quite other message. Is Bishop suggesting that it is more often
than not the Church which clouds the vision, and by its excessive talk of sin
and its consequences prevents the glory all around us from being seen?

This celestial seascape, with white herons got up as angels,
flying as high as they want and as far as they want sidewise
in tiers and tiers of immaculate reflections;
the whole region, from the highest heron
down to the weightless mangrove island
with bright green leaves edged neatly with bird-droppings
like illumination in silver,
and down to the suggestively Gothic arches of the mangrove
    roots

and the beautiful pea-green back-pasture
where occasionally a fish jumps, like a wild-flower
in an ornamental spray of spray;
this cartoon by Raphael for a tapestry for a Pope:
it does look like heaven.
But a skeletal lighthouse standing there
in black and white clerical dress,
who lives on his nerves, thinks he knows better.
He thinks that hell rages below his iron feet,
that that is why the shallow water is so warm,
and he knows that heaven is not like this.
Heaven is not like flying or swimming,
but has something to do with blackness and a strong glare
and when it gets dark he will remember something
strongly worded to say on the subject.

Elizabeth Bishop (1911–79), 'Seascape'.

The imagination fettered

Blake held orthodox Christianity responsible for clouding what he calls
elsewhere 'the visions of eternity', though even then 'we see only as it were
the hems of their garments / When with our vegetable eyes we view these
wondrous visions'. In his poem *Milton* John Milton is blamed: his Christianity, Blake argues, was compromised by his high regard for the heroic values
of classical epic. Ololon is Blake's personification of the female aspects of
Milton's psyche, not properly integrated into his being because of this
failure. Beulah, mentioned in passing in Scripture (Isa 62:4), first achieved
prominence when used by Bunyan to describe the pleasant land in which
the pilgrims rested before crossing the River of Death to enter heaven.
Blake uses it here as a place mistaken for heaven, to portray the heavy price
Milton paid for his fettered imagination. 'The effluence divine' is everywhere about us, will we but open our eyes. Though, like the Israelites, we
are kept from the promised land by evils personified as the great biblical
giants, Og and Anak (Deut 3 and 9), even the scent of the smallest flower
contains eternity. As Blake expresses it more simply in the lyric 'Auguries of
Innocence': 'To see a world in a grain of sand, / And a heaven in a wild
flower, / Hold infinity in the palm of your hand, / And eternity in an hour'. Is
it not, then, all too easy to exaggerate the negative side of the human
condition, as, Blake implies, Milton did in *Paradise Lost*?

Thou perceivest the flowers put forth their precious odours,
And none can tell how from so small a centre comes such
sweets,
Forgetting that within that centre Eternity expands

Its ever-during doors, that Og and Anak fiercely guard.
First, ere the morning breaks, joy opens in the flowery
        bosoms,
Joy even to tears, which the sun rising dries. First the wild
        thyme,
And meadowsweet downy and soft, waving among the
        reeds,
Light springing on the air, lead the sweet dance. They wake
The honeysuckle sleeping on the oak. The flaunting beauty
Revels along upon the wind. The white-thorn, lovely may,
Opens her many lovely eyes. Listening, the rose still sleeps;
None dare to wake her. Soon she burst her crimson-curtained
        bed,
And comes forth in the majesty of beauty. Every flower –
The pink, the jessamine, the wall-flower, the carnation,
The jonquil, the mild lily – opes her heavens. Every tree
And flower and herb soon fill the air with an innumerable
        dance,
Yet all in order sweet and lovely. Men are sick with love.
Such is a vision of the lamentation of Beulah over Ololon.

                    William Blake (1757–1827), from *Milton*, Book 2.

Childhood wonder

In this poem Elizabeth Jennings raises a different issue about perception.
How far is our awareness of God's involvement in the world affected, not by
distraction through 'trade' (Hopkins), nor by loss of childhood innocence
(Traherne), nor by the Church's preoccupation with sin (Bishop, Blake)
but by a lack of wonder, even at what is frightening or threatening? Because
we can, in a narrow sense, 'understand' natural phenomena we vainly
suppose ourselves in control of our world, but for a young boy, as for ancient
peoples, thunder is a revelation of God. That Jennings takes as her example
what in many evokes fear is witness to the strength of her Catholic faith;
despite much suffering in her life she refuses to confine God's presence to
nature's gentler aspects.

        That great bubble of silence, almost tangible quiet was
                shattered. There was no prelude, the huge chords
        Broke and sounded timpani over the town, and then lightning,
                first darting, then strong bars
            Taking hold of the sky, taking hold of us as we sank into
                primitive people,
        Wondering at and frightened of the elements, forgetting so
                swiftly how naming had once seemed

To give them into our hands. Not any longer. We were
    powerless now completely.

But today we have risen with the rain and, though it is
    torrential, we believe at moments that we
Still have power over that. We are wrong. Those birds escap-
    ing through showers show us
They are more imperial than we are. We shift, talk, doze,
    look at papers,
Though one child is remembering how last night he stood
    with defiance

And joy at his window and shouted, 'Do it again, God, do it
    again!',
Can we say he was less wise than us? We cannot. He acknow-
    ledged Zeus,
Thor, God the Father, and was prepared to cheer or dispute
    with any of them.
This afternoon he watches the sky, praying the night will show
    God's strength again
And he, without fear, feel those drums beating and bursting
    through his defended, invisible mind.

    Elizabeth Jennings (b. 1926), 'Thunder and a Boy' from *Growing Points*.

Happy without a mate

Marvell lived through the English Civil War and subsequent Common-
wealth. A personal friend of Milton, he secured his release from prison
under Charles II and, as MP for Hull for almost twenty years (1659–78), was
a passionate advocate of religious toleration as well as a fierce critic of
government policy. A contemporary of Traherne, it was perhaps his experience of these turbulent times which led him to use the same image – Eden
– in a different way, to suggest the superiority of nature over humanity:
'society is all but rude [compared] to this delicious solitude'. Men deck
themselves with garlands, and lovers carve their names on trees, little
realizing their own inferiority. The music of the divine is lodged in the very
trees, as the classical myths illustrate. Apollo pursued human beauty in
Daphne, but instead received the laurel, sign of poetry; Pan pursued Syrinx,
but instead obtained the reed, from which musical pipes are made. Marvell
even humorously supposes that love of nature, not sexual desire, was the
gods' driving force. A similar humour leads us out of the poem's central
vision. Alone in the garden Marvell has ecstatic experiences inspired by the
natural world, as he imagines Adam did in Eden: in fact, Eve was needed,
not as a companion, but to allay the pleasures of solitude.

How vainly men themselves amaze
To win the palm, the oak, or bays,
And their uncessant labours see
Crowned from some single herb or tree,
Whose short and narrow vergèd shade
Does prudently their toils upbraid,
While all flowers and all trees do close
To weave the garlands of repose.

Fair Quiet, have I found thee here,
And Innocence, thy sister dear!
Mistaken long, I sought you then
In busy companies of men.
Your sacred plants, if here below,
Only among the plants will grow.
Society is all but rude,
To this delicious solitude.

No white nor red was ever seen
So amorous as this lovely green.
Fond lovers, cruel as their flame,
Cut in these trees their mistress' name.
Little, alas, they know, or heed,
How far these beauties hers exceed!
Fair trees! wheres'e'er your barks I wound,
No name shall but your own be found.

When we have run our passion's heat,
Love hither makes his best retreat.
The gods, that mortal beauty chase,
Still in a tree did end their race.
Apollo hunted Daphne so,
Only that she might laurel grow.
And Pan did after Syrinx speed,
Not as a nymph, but for a reed. . . .

Here at the fountain's sliding foot,
Or at some fruit-tree's mossy root,
Casting the body's vest aside,
My soul into the boughs does glide:
There like a bird it sits, and sings,
Then whets, and combs its silver wings,
And, till prepared for longer flight,
Waves in its plumes the various light.

> Such was that happy garden-state,
> While man there walked without a mate:
> After a place so pure, and sweet,
> What other help could yet be meet!
> But 'twas beyond a mortal's share
> To wander solitary there:
> Two paradises 'twere in one
> To live in paradise alone.
>
> Andrew Marvell (1621–78), from 'The Garden'.

The power of experience

As Marvell reminded us, nature does not need human beings to make it sacramental: God can be present in nature, even if none of us are around to view it. Nonetheless, the sense of nature as a participatory sign of something greater than itself is clearly enhanced by human perception, and for many this enhancement comes through some powerful experience. Called by Wordsworth a 'Poem on the Growth of a Poet's Mind', *The Prelude* is deliberately autobiographical. Here we have the last of the visionary moments it records. These, as Wordsworth called them, 'spots of time' had for him permanent significance; when recollected, they could restore to a mind depressed by the mundane a sense of other, wider possibilities. His account of climbing Mount Snowdon to see the sun rise begins with ordinary details of the climb; it then passes from a sudden visionary moment into a passage of reflection in which Wordsworth draws out from what he has seen its spiritual significance. The landscape is sacramental in the sense that it is an image of the highest powers of the mind, which are themselves an 'intimation' of the nature of God. To be aware of this, for Wordsworth as for Traherne, transforms every aspect of life.

> I looked about, and lo!
> The moon stood naked in the heavens, at height
> Immense above my head, and on the shore
> I found myself of a huge sea of mist,
> Which, meek and silent, rested at my feet:
> A hundred hills their dusky backs upheaved
> All over this still ocean, and beyond,
> Far, far beyond, the vapours shot themselves,
> In headlands, tongues, and promontory shapes,
> Into the sea, the real sea, that seemed
> To dwindle, and give up its majesty,
> Usurped upon as far as sight could reach.
> Meanwhile, the moon looked down upon this show
> In single glory, and we stood, the mist

Touching our very feet; and from the shore
At distance not the third part of a mile
Was a blue chasm, a fracture in the vapour,
A deep and gloomy breathing-place, through which
Mounted the roar of waters, torrents, streams
Innumerable, roaring with one voice.
The universal spectacle throughout
Was shaped for admiration and delight,
Grand in itself alone, but in that breach
Through which the homeless voice of waters rose,
That dark deep thoroughfare had Nature lodged
The Soul, the Imagination of the whole.

    A meditation rose in me that night
Upon the lonely mountain when the scene
Had passed away, and it appeared to me
The perfect image of a mighty mind,
Of one that feeds upon infinity,
That is exalted by an underpresence,
The sense of God, or whatsoe'er is dim
Or vast in its own being: above all
One function of such mind had Nature there
Exhibited by putting forth, and that
With circumstance most awful and sublime,
That domination which she oftentimes
Exerts upon the outward face of things,
So moulds them, and endues, abstracts, combines,
Or by abrupt and unhabitual influence
Doth make one object so impress itself
Upon all others, and pervade them so,
That even the grossest minds must see and hear
And cannot choose but feel. The power which these
Acknowledge when thus moved, which Nature thus
Thrusts forth upon the senses, is the express
Resemblance, in the fulness of its strength
Made visible, a genuine counterpart
And brother of the glorious faculty
Which higher minds bear with them as their own.
That is the very spirit in which they deal
With all the objects of the universe;
They from their native selves can send abroad
Like transformations, for themselves create
A like existence, and, whene'er it is

Created for them, catch it by an instinct.
Them the enduring and the transient both
Serve to exalt; they build up greatest things
From least suggestions, ever on the watch,
Willing to work and to be wrought upon.
They need not extraordinary calls
To rouse them: in a world of life they live,
By sensible impressions not enthralled,
But quickened, roused, and made thereby more fit
To hold communion with the invisible world.
Such minds are truly from the Deity,
For they are powers; and hence the highest bliss
That can be known is theirs, the consciousness
Of whom they are habitually infused
Through every image, and through every thought,
And all impressions; hence religion, faith,
And endless occupation for the soul,
Whether discursive or intuitive;
Hence sovereignty within and peace at will,
Emotion which best foresight need not fear,
Most worthy then of trust when most intense.
Hence cheerfulness in every act of life,
Hence truth in moral judgements, and delight
That fails not in the external universe.

William Wordsworth (1770–1850), from *The Prelude* (1805),
Book 13.

An unseen shadow

Shelley, like Wordsworth, reflects the Romantic movement's concern with experience. Because he was expelled from Oxford in 1811 for his pamphlet *The Necessity of Atheism*, it is easy to assume that he was totally hostile to religion. But in fact he maintained an interest throughout his life, and, as this poem, written five years after the pamphlet, illustrates, it seems to have been the form of organized religion to which he took most exception, rather than religious experience as such. By 'intellectual' Shelley means immaterial or spiritual. While rejecting the 'poisonous names' by which the divine has been traditionally identified, he feels that his experience leaves him in no doubt about the reality of a divine Spirit. Though it reveals itself only obliquely through the natural and human worlds, life is meaningless unless we perceive this numinous presence.

The awful shadow of some unseen Power
  Floats though unseen amongst us, – visiting

This various world with as inconstant wing
As summer winds that creep from flower to flower. –
Like moonbeams that behind some piny mountain shower,
 It visits with inconstant glance
 Each human heart and countenance;
Like hues and harmonies of evening, –
 Like clouds in starlight widely spread, –
 Like memory of music fled, –
 Like aught that for its grace may be
Dear, and yet dearer for its mystery. ...

No voice from some sublimer world hath ever
 To sage or poet these responses given –
 Therefore the name of God and ghosts and Heaven,
Remain the records of their vain endeavour,
Frail spells – whose uttered charm might not avail to sever,
 From all we hear and all we see,
 Doubt, chance, and mutability.
Thy light alone – like mist o'er mountains driven,
 Or music by the night wind sent
 Through strings of some still instrument,
 Or moonlight on a midnight stream,
Gives grace and truth to life's unquiet dream.

Love, Hope, and Self-esteem, like clouds depart
 And come, for some uncertain moments lent.
 Man were immortal, and omnipotent,
Didst thou, unknown and awful as thou art,
Keep with thy glorious train firm state within his heart
 Thou messenger of sympathies,
 That wax and wane in lovers' eyes –
Thou – that to human thought art nourishment,
 Like darkness to a dying flame!
 Depart not as thy shadow came,
 Depart not – lest the grave should be,
Like life and fear, a dark reality.
  Percy Bysshe Shelley (1792–1822), from 'Hymn to Intellectual Beauty'.

Nature's cathedral

Worship can be sacramental, whether or not specific sacraments are also
involved. This has been a repeated theme throughout Christian history, for
in worship we can share in the adoration of heaven. Less frequent is the
notion, as in this sonnet by Longfellow, of nature (such as in his local state

of Maine) also offering its appropriate worship. The trunk-like appearance
of the heavy pillars of Romanesque architecture has often led to compar-
isons between forest and cathedral church; Longfellow reverses the
comparison, and with his choice of title, 'My Cathedral', leaves us in no
doubt which he prefers.

> Like two cathedral towers these stately pines
>   Uplift their fretted summits tipped with cones;
>   The arch beneath them is not built with stones –
>   Not Art but Nature traced these lovely lines,
> And carved this graceful arabesque of vines;
>   No organ but the wind here sighs and moans,
>   No sepulchre conceals a martyr's bones,
>   No marble bishop on his tomb reclines.
> Enter! the pavement, carpeted with leaves,
>   Gives back a softened echo to thy tread!
>   Listen! the choir is singing; all the birds,
> In leafy galleries beneath the eaves,
>   Are singing! listen, ere the sound be fled,
>   And learn there may be worship without words.
>   Henry Wadsworth Longfellow (1807–82), 'My Cathedral'.

Even the ravens have their say

Educated at Durham and Cambridge, Christopher or 'Kit' Smart led a
troubled life, suffering from bouts of insanity and ending his life in a
debtors' prison. Throughout, however, his love of nature is evident, even if
at times this took eccentric forms – in profusely addressing flowers or his
cat. In this extract from one of his longer poems we find Longfellow's theme
repeated. All the birds sing in choir, even the ravens with 'their throats'
coarse ruttling', as part of a hymn of grateful praise to their creator.

> Immense Creator! whose all-pow'rful hand
> Framed universal Being, and whose eye
> Saw like thyself, that all things formed were good;
> Where shall the tim'rous bard thy praise begin,
> Where end the purest sacrifice of song,
> And just thanksgiving? – The thought-kindling light,
> Thy prime production, darts upon my mind
> Its vivifying beams, my heart illumines,
> And fills my soul with gratitude and Thee.
> Hail to the cheerful rays of ruddy morn,
> That paint the streaky east, and blithsome rouse
> The birds, the cattle, and mankind from rest! ...

Without thy aid, without thy gladsome beams
The tribes of woodland warblers would remain
Mute on the bending branches, nor recite
The praise of him, who, ere he formed their lord,
Their voices tuned to transport, winged their flight,
And bade them call for nurture, and receive;
And lo! they call; the blackbird and the thrush,
The woodlark, and the redbreast jointly call;
He hears, and feeds their feathered families,
He feeds his sweet musicians, – nor neglects
Th' invoking ravens in the greenwood wide;
And tho' their throats' coarse ruttling hurt the ear,
They mean it all for music, thanks and praise.

> Christopher Smart (1722–71), from 'On the Goodness of the
> Supreme Being'.

Spring light

Born to a wealthy legal family in Amherst, Massachusetts, already by her mid-twenties Emily Dickinson had adopted the life of a recluse. Only seven of her poems were published during her lifetime. It is a poetry which shows the influence of the American Transcendentalist movement: passionate and non-conformist, it is often religious in feeling and content, though Dickinson herself belonged to no church. In reflecting on the power and majesty of God, it is tempting to suppose nature at its most spectacular as most indicative of his presence. But here Dickinson suggests that the gentle play of light in spring can be just as sacramental as a huge mountain or mighty waterfall. It evokes an awe which no scientific explanation can account for, though human commerce or 'trade' (recall Hopkins' earlier aspersions) may interrupt the feeling of wonder.

A light exists in spring
Not present on the year
At any other period,
When March is scarcely here;

A colour stands abroad
On solitary fields
That science cannot overtake,
But human nature feels.

It waits upon the lawn,
It shows the furthest tree;
Upon the furthest slope you know
It almost speaks to you.

Then as horizons step,
Or noons report away,
Without the formula of sound,
It passes and we stay –

A quality of loss
Affecting our content,
As trade had suddenly encroached
Upon a sacrament.

Emily Dickinson (1830–86), c. 1864.

WATERS OF LIFE

Introduction

It is not only the natural world that reflects the divine character: the divine also finds special focus in particular material elements operating within our human world. Though water can of course have a threatening or frightening aspect (floods or the raging sea), the first thought that surely comes to mind is either of its cleansing or of its refreshing qualities. To this day Muslims use water as a symbol: cleansing the body before prayer is a sign of desire for interior purification. That too seems to have been the motivation with John the Baptist (the word Baptist literally means someone who dips or plunges under water). We are told that he preached 'a baptism of repentance for the forgiveness of sins' (Mark 1:4). However, the New Testament is careful to distinguish this baptism from that of Jesus, which conveys the gift of the Spirit (e.g. Mark 1:8). So to the backward-looking image of cleansing from sin there was now added a new forward-looking emphasis which the Spirit makes possible: the water is refreshing or transforming. With this came also the idea that the water was more than a sign: that, mysteriously, it was the way of transformation by the Spirit. God acts through the water to create a new creature: it is this understanding which turns the water from sign to something sacramental.

That image of a new creation through baptism is reflected in Jesus' baptism in the River Jordan (described below by Milton). It is an emphasis which is particularly strong in John's Gospel, as in the dialogue with Nicodemus, with its allusions to the need to be 'born anew' and 'of water and the Spirit' (John 3:3 and 5). Paul too has a strong forward-looking element: 'We were buried with him by baptism into death, so that as Christ was raised from the dead ... we too might walk in newness of life' (Rom 6:4). This is the stress we find reflected in Law and Coleridge. Nonetheless, the backward-looking understanding of baptism as release from sin continued to play an important role, particularly as Augustine developed Romans 5:12–17 into the notion of 'original sin', the idea that there is in each newly born child an innate tendency towards sin, release from which can only be secured by the divine grace given through baptism. George Herbert's subtle treatment of this theme is followed by a number of other passages, both comic (e.g. Edmund Gosse) and serious (e.g. Thomas Hardy), which illustrate the range of the Christian debate both on original sin and on infant baptism. The final group of extracts focuses on the question of how baptismal imagery may be most effectively employed. Is it a case of 'the more, the merrier' (Keble)? What is the effect when water is juxtaposed with other, equally powerful symbols such as blood (Melville) or fire (Vaughan)? Or does the water on its own say it all (Flannery O'Connor)?

The dove descends

Here Milton puts into Satan's mouth a description of the work of John the Baptist and in particular his baptism of Jesus. The past reference of John's baptism ('wash off sin') clearly would not do as an account of what happened to Christ, if he truly were sinless. So, following the Gospel accounts (e.g. Matt 3:13–17), Milton places the emphasis elsewhere. The 'dove' descends to mark a new creation, just as the Spirit 'hovered' at the first creation (Gen 1:2) and again at the renewal of the world after the Flood (Gen 8:6–12). Milton's use of 'stream' is not accidental. In *Paradise Lost* (XII, 442), he speaks of 'the profluent stream'; while in his *Christian Doctrine* (ch. 28) he explains that flowing water must be used, perhaps to suggest adequately the possibility of regeneration and new life.

> This ill news I bring, the woman's seed
> Destined to this, is late of woman born.
> His birth to our just fear gave no small cause,
> But his growth now to youth's full flower, displaying
> All virtue, grace and wisdom to achieve
> Things highest, greatest, multiplies my fear.
> Before him a great prophet, to proclaim
> His coming, is sent harbinger, who all
> Invites, and in the consecrated stream
> Pretends to wash off sin, and fit them so
> Purified to receive him pure, or rather
> To do him honour as their king; all come,
> And he himself among them was baptized,
> Not thence to be more pure, but to receive
> The testimony of heaven, that who he is
> Thenceforth the nations may not doubt; I saw
> The prophet do him reverence, on him rising
> Out of the water, heaven above the clouds
> Unfold her crystal doors, thence on his head
> A perfect dove descend, whate'er it meant,

And out of heaven the sovereign voice I heard,
This is my son beloved, in him am pleased.

John Milton (1608–74), from *Paradise Regained*, Book I.

A new birth

William Law was one of the most influential religious writers of his day: his best-known work, *A Serious Call to a Devout and Holy Life* of 1728, was praised by figures as different as John Wesley and Samuel Johnson. In later life Law's writings took an increasingly mystical turn. This extract is drawn from one of these, published in 1757 and destined to go through seven editions in the next half century. Here not only is the imagery of new birth to the fore, as in John's Gospel, but it is also linked, through the story of the creation of humanity in the divine image in Genesis (1:26), with John's notion of the Father, Son and Holy Spirit indwelling the Christian believer (14:15–20; 17:18–23).

> Our baptism is to signify our seeking and obtaining a new birth. And our being baptized in, or into the name of the Father, Son, and Holy Ghost, tells us in the plainest manner, what birth it is that we seek, namely, such a new birth as may make us again what we were at first, a living real image or offspring of the Father, Son, and Holy Ghost.
>
> It is owned on all hands, that we are baptized into a renovation of some divine birth that we had lost; and that we may not be at a loss to know what that divine birth is, the form in baptism openly declares to us, that it is to regain that first birth of Father, Son, and Holy Ghost in our souls, which at the first made us to be truly and really images of the nature of the Holy Trinity in Unity. The form in baptism is but very imperfectly apprehended, till it is understood to have this great meaning in it. And it must be owned, that the scriptures tend wholly to guide us to this understanding of it. For since they teach us a birth of God, a birth of the Spirit, that we must obtain, and that baptism, the appointed sacrament of this new birth, is to be done in the name of the Father, Son, and Holy Ghost, can there be any doubt, that this sacrament is to signify the renovation of the birth of the Holy Trinity in our souls? ...
>
> What an harmonious agreement does there thus appear, between our creation and redemption? and how finely, how surprisingly do our first and our second birth answer to, and illustrate one another?

William Law (1686–1761), from *Christian Regeneration*.

Death dies

Law's image of God himself indwelling us and thus effecting our transformation is used with particular poignancy in this sonnet by Coleridge. He
added a note to explain that it was 'composed on a sick-bed, under severe
bodily suffering, on my spiritual birthday, October 28th'; hence its original
title, 'My Baptismal Birthday'. Such information gives additional point to
the imagery with which he begins: baptism is not merely adoption alongside
Christ as God's Son (Rom 8:15 AV); it is incorporation into Christ's very
being (Rom 6:1–11; Gal 2:20), such that death itself now no longer has
dominion over him: 'as in Adam all die, so in Christ shall all be made alive'
(1 Cor 15:22).

> God's child in Christ adopted, – Christ my all, –
> What that earth boasts were not lost cheaply, rather
> Than forfeit that blest name, by which I call
> The Holy One, the Almighty God, my Father? –
> Father! in Christ we live, and Christ in Thee –
> Eternal Thou, and everlasting we.
> The heir of heaven, henceforth I fear not death:
> In Christ I live! in Christ I draw the breath
> Of the true life! – Let then earth, sea, and sky
> Make war against me! On my heart I show
> Their mighty master's seal. In vain they try
> To end my life, that can but end its woe. –
> Is that a death-bed where a Christian lies? –
> Yes! but not his – 'tis Death itself there dies.
>
> Samuel Taylor Coleridge (1772–1834), 'My Baptismal Birthday'.

O blessed streams!

After a brilliant career at Cambridge it looked as though George Herbert
was set for major public advancement, but he abandoned this for the parish
ministry, serving as rector of Bemerton in Wiltshire for the last three years
of his life. In the following poem, though the primary focus, unlike that of
Law or Coleridge, is on the other, retrospective effect of baptism – the
washing away of sin – Herbert insists that baptism also carries with it
implications for the future in refreshment and new life. For him this is a
deliverance which continues into the present, and is thus not exclusively
concerned with the removal of original sin. At baptism Herbert's name was
written in God's Book of Life (Rev 21:27), and so ultimate victory over the
forces of evil was assured. The sacramental character of that final victory is
underlined through the connecting image of the water. John 19:34 had
described how water flowed from Christ's side at the Crucifixion. Herbert

imaginatively envisages that stream continuing to flow from heaven, acting through the waters of baptism to restrain our tendency towards sin or else to provoke tears of penitence.

> As he that sees a dark and shady grove
>> Stays not, but looks beyond it on the sky,
>> So when I view my sins, mine eyes remove
> More backward still, and to that water fly
> Which is above the heav'ns, whose spring and rent
>> Is in my dear Redeemer's piercèd side.
>> O blessèd streams! either ye do prevent
> And stop our sins from growing thick and wide,
> Or else give tears to drown them as they grow.
>> In you Redemption measures all my time,
>> And spreads the plaster equal to the crime:
> You taught the Book of Life my name, that so,
>> Whatever future sins should me miscall,
>> Your first acquaintance might discredit all.

George Herbert (1593–1633), 'Holy Baptism' from *The Temple*.

Dripping and spluttering

Herbert wrote a companion to the preceding poem which confronts an objection commonly raised in this time against infant baptism – that infants cannot consciously put their faith in Christ when they are baptized. One answer to this might be to claim that even infants have original sin which needs to be washed away. A stronger argument, and one accepted by almost all Christians, is that before we do anything God is already at work seeking to elicit our response and ultimate salvation. Nonetheless, some have argued that both loyalty to the Scriptures and a proper stress on human responsibility require confinement of baptism to adults. This is the view taken by Plymouth Brethren, the sect among whom Edmund Gosse was brought up. In adopting the practice of complete immersion, Plymouth Brethren continue what had been the custom for infants in the Western Church throughout the Middle Ages, and remains the practice within Orthodoxy to this day.

> . My public baptism was the central event of my whole child-
> hood. Everything, since the earliest dawn of consciousness,
> seemed to have been leading up to it. Everything, afterwards,
> seemed to be leading down and away from it. The practice of
> immersing communicants on the sea-beach at Oddicombe had
> now been completely abandoned, but we possessed as yet no
> tank for a baptismal purpose in our own Room. The Room in the

adjoining town, however, was really quite a large chapel, and it was amply provided with the needful conveniences. It was our practice, therefore, at this time, to claim the hospitality of our neighbours. Baptisms were made an occasion for friendly relations between the two congregations, and led to pleasant social intercourse. I believe that the ministers and elders of the two meetings arranged to combine their forces at these times, and to baptize communicants from both congregations.

The minister of the town meeting was Mr S., a very handsome old gentleman, of venerable and powerful appearance. He had snowy hair and a long white beard, but from under shaggy eyebrows there blazed out great black eyes which warned the beholder that the snow was an ornament and not a sign of decrepitude. The eve of my baptism at length drew near; it was fixed for October 12, almost exactly three weeks after my tenth birthday. I was dressed in old clothes, and a suit of smarter things was packed up in a carpet-bag. After nightfall, this carpet-bag, accompanied by my Father, myself, Miss Marks and Mary Grace, was put in a four-wheeled cab, and driven, a long way in the dark, to the chapel of our friends. There we were received, in a blaze of lights, with a pressure of hands, with a murmur of voices, with ejaculations and even with tears, and were conducted, amid unspeakable emotion, to places of honour in the front row of the congregation.

The scene was one which would have been impressive, not merely to such hermits as we were, but even to worldly persons accustomed to life and to its curious and variegated experiences. To me it was dazzling beyond words, inexpressibly exciting, an initiation to every kind of publicity and glory. There were many candidates, but the rest of them, – mere grown-up men and women, – gave thanks aloud that it was their privilege to follow where I led. I was the acknowledged hero of the hour. Those were days when newspaper enterprise was scarcely in its infancy, and the event owed nothing to journalistic effort. In spite of that, the news of this remarkable ceremony, the immersion of a little boy of ten years old 'as an adult', had spread far and wide through the county in the course of three weeks. The chapel of our hosts was, as I have said, very large; it was commonly too large for their needs, but on this night it was crowded to the ceiling, and the crowd had come – as every soft murmur assured me – to see *me*. ...

In the centre of the chapel-floor a number of planks had been taken up, and revealed a pool which might have been supposed to be a small swimming-bath. We gazed down into this dark square of mysterious waters, from the tepid surface of which faint swirls of vapour rose. The whole congregation was arranged, tier above tier, about the four straight sides of this pool; every person was able to see what happened in it without any unseemly struggling or standing on forms. Mr S. now rose, an impressive hieratic figure, commanding attention and imploring perfect silence. ...

Mr S. proposed to the congregation a hymn, which was long enough to occupy them during the preparations for the actual baptism. He then retired to the vestry, and I (for I was to be the first to testify) was led by Miss Marks and Mary Grace into the species of tent of which I have just spoken. Its pale sides seemed to shake with the jubilant singing of the saints outside, while part of my clothing was removed and I was prepared for immersion. A sudden cessation of the hymn warned us that the Minister was now ready, and we emerged into the glare of lights and faces to find Mr S. already standing in the water up to his knees. Feeling as small as one of our microscopical specimens, almost infinitesimally tiny as I descended into his Titanic arms, I was handed down the steps to him. He was dressed in a kind of long surplice, underneath which – as I could not, even in that moment, help observing – the air gathered in long bubbles which he strove to flatten out. The end of his noble beard he had tucked away; his shirt-sleeves were turned up at the wrist.

The entire congregation was now silent, so silent that the uncertain splashing of my feet as I descended seemed to deafen me. Mr S., a little embarrassed by my short stature, succeeded at length in securing me with one palm on my chest and the other between my shoulders. He said, slowly, in a loud, sonorous voice that seemed to enter my brain and empty it, 'I baptize thee, my Brother, in the name of the Father and of the Son and of the Holy Ghost!' Having intoned this formula, he then gently flung me backwards until I was wholly under the water, and then – as he brought me up again, and tenderly steadied my feet on the steps of the font, and delivered me, dripping and spluttering, into the anxious hands of the women, who hurried me to the tent – the whole assembly broke forth in a thunder of song, a paean of praise to God for this manifestation of his marvellous goodness and mercy. So great was the enthusiasm, that it could hardly be restrained so as to allow the other candidates, the humdrum adults who followed in my wet and glorious footsteps, to undergo a ritual about which, in their case, no one in the congregation pretended to be able to take even the most languid interest. ...

I would fain close this remarkable episode on a key of solemnity, but alas! if I am to be loyal to the truth, I must record that some of the other little boys presently complained to Mary Grace that I put out my tongue at them in mockery, during the service in the Room, to remind them that I now broke bread as one of the Saints and that they did not.

Edmund Gosse (1849–1928), Father and Son, chapter 8.

Funereal tears

Infant baptism is, of course, equally capable of generating humorous scenarios. Dickens here parodies some of the worst features of private baptism in the nineteenth-century Church of England. 'Little Paul' is waiting to be baptized in a gloomy church, while the vicar deals with another group of parishioners seeking marriage. Legend has it that cries at baptism are of the devil coming out of the child, but here the funereal atmosphere suggests that to Paul the figure in white is a ghost.

Once upon the road to church, Mr Dombey clapped his hands for the amusement of his son. At which instance of parental enthusiasm Miss Tox was enchanted. But exclusive of this incident, the chief difference between the christening party and a party in a mourning coach consisted in the colours of the carriage and horses.

Arrived at the church steps, they were received by a portentous beadle. Mr Dombey dismounting first to help the ladies out, and standing near him at the church door, looked like another beadle. A beadle less gorgeous but more dreadful; the beadle of private life; the beadle of our business and our bosoms.

Miss Tox's hand trembled as she slipped it through Mr Dombey's arm, and felt herself escorted up the steps, preceded by a cocked hat and a Babylonian collar. It seemed for a moment like that other solemn institution, 'Wilt thou have this man, Lucretia?' 'Yes, I will.'

'Please to bring the child in quick out of the air there,' whispered the beadle, holding open the inner door of the church.

Little Paul might have asked with Hamlet 'into my grave?' so chill and earthy was the place. The tall shrouded pulpit and reading desk; the dreary perspective of empty pews stretching away under the galleries, and empty benches mounting to the

roof and lost in the shadow of the great grim organ; the dusty
matting and cold stone slabs; the grisly free seats in the aisles;
and the damp corner by the bell-rope, where the black trestles
used for funerals were stowed away, along with some shovels
and baskets, and a coil or two of deadly-looking rope; the
strange, unusual, uncomfortable smell, and the cadaverous
light; were all in unison. It was a cold and dismal scene. . . .

After another cold interval, a wheezy little pew-opener afflic-
ted with an asthma, appropriate to the churchyard, if not to the
church, summoned them to the font – a rigid marble basin
which seemed to have been playing a churchyard game at cup
and ball with its matter of fact pedestal, and to have been just
that moment caught on the top of it. Here they waited some little
time while the marriage party enrolled themselves; and mean-
while the wheezy little pew-opener – partly in consequence of
her infirmity, and partly that the marriage party might not forget
her – went about the building coughing like a grampus.

Presently the clerk (the only cheerful-looking object there,
and *he* was an undertaker) came up with a jug of warm water,
and said something, as he poured it into the font, about taking
the chill off; which millions of gallons boiling hot could not have
done for the occasion. Then the clergyman, an amiable and
mild-looking young curate, but obviously afraid of the baby,
appeared like the principal character in a ghost-story, 'a tall
figure all in white;' at sight of whom Paul rent the air with his
cries, and never left off again till he was taken out black in the
face.

Charles Dickens (1812–70), *Dombey and Son*, chapter 5.

Even cats have souls

Here a contemporary Anglican, P. D. James, mocks the sentimentality
which so often goes with infant baptism. Though she is best known as a
detective writer, in this case we have a novel set in the year 2021, with the
human race apparently soon to die out, the last human being having been
born 25 years earlier.

The christening party was coming up the path, the old man,
now wearing a stole, shepherding them with small cries of
encouragement. There were two middle-aged women and two
older men, the men soberly dressed in blue suits, the women
wearing flowered hats, incongruous above their winter coats.
Each of the women was carrying a white bundle wrapped in a
shawl beneath which fell the lace-trimmed pleated folds of

SIGNS OF GRACE

christening robes. Theo made to pass them, eyes tactfully averted, but the two women almost barred his way and, smiling the meaningless smile of the half-demented, thrust forward the bundles, inviting his admiration. The two kittens, ears flattened beneath the ribboned bonnets, looked both ridiculous and endearing. Their eyes were wide-open, uncomprehending opal pools, and they seemed unworried at their confinement. He wondered if they had been drugged, then decided that they had probably been handled, caressed and carried like babies since birth and were accustomed to it. He wondered, too, about the priest. Whether validly ordained or an impostor – and there were plenty about – he was hardly engaged in an orthodox rite. The Church of England, no longer with a common doctrine or a common liturgy, was so fragmented that there was no knowing what some sects might not have come to believe, but he doubted whether the christening of animals was encouraged. The new Archbishop, who described herself as a Christian Rationalist, would, he suspected, have prohibited infant baptism on the grounds of superstition, had infant baptism still been possible. But she could hardly control what was happening in every redundant church. The kittens presumably would not welcome a douche of cold water over their heads, but no one else was likely to object. The charade was a fitting conclusion to a morning of folly. He set off walking vigorously towards sanity and that empty inviolate house he called home.

P. D. James (b. 1920), *The Children of Men*, chapter 8.

Sorrow's campaign against sin

Objections to infant baptism are by no means confined to the sentimentality which it sometimes engenders. The theology behind it has been seen as deeply uncharitable, even evil. Though in his youth Hardy had considered ordination, long before *Tess of the d'Urbervilles* appeared in 1893 he had lost his faith and this had been replaced by a bleak conception of life as a battle against a hostile world. Tess's misfortunes begin when she is seduced by Alec d'Urberville. In this extract she seeks to baptize their child herself, in the hope that thereby its eternal salvation may be secured. In his depiction of Tess's fears Hardy is unfair to the Christianity of his day since the traditional view then and in previous centuries was that only actual sin merited hell-fire, whereas the original sin of an unbaptized infant merely precluded the full bliss of heaven. Similarly later in the chapter when the parson is asked whether baptism by Tess is sufficient, Hardy tells us that 'the man and the ecclesiastic fought within him, and the victory fell to the man', whereas every branch of Christianity has always considered baptism by a lay person as valid in cases of necessity. Nevertheless, Hardy does provide an effective critique, not so much of traditional doctrine, as of popular suppositions which often went unchecked and gave rise to cruel fears. This critique is made the more pathetic by Tess calling the child after God's curse on childbirth in Genesis (3:16).

> When Tess reached home it was to learn to her grief that the baby had been suddenly taken ill since the afternoon. Some such collapse had been probable, so tender and puny was its frame; but the event came as a shock nevertheless.
>
> The baby's offence against society in coming into the world was forgotten by the girl-mother; her soul's desire was to continue that offence by preserving the life of the child. However, it soon grew clear that the hour of emancipation for that little prisoner of the flesh was to arrive earlier than her worst misgivings had conjectured. And when she had discovered this she was plunged into a misery which transcended that of the child's simple loss. Her baby had not been baptized.
>
> Tess had drifted into a frame of mind which accepted passively the consideration that if she should have to burn for what she had done, burn she must, and there was an end of it. Like all village girls she was well grounded in the Holy Scriptures, and had dutifully studied the histories of Aholah and Aholibah [Ezek 23], and knew the inferences to be drawn therefrom. But when the same question arose with regard to the baby, it had a very different colour. Her darling was about to die, and no salvation. ...
>
> In her misery she rocked herself upon the bed. The clock struck the solemn hour of one, that hour when fancy stalks outside reason, and malignant possibilities stand rock-firm as facts. She thought of the child consigned to the nethermost corner of hell, as its double doom for lack of baptism and lack of legitimacy; saw the arch-fiend tossing it with his three-pronged fork, like the one they used for heating the oven on baking days; to which picture she added many other quaint and curious details of torment sometimes taught the young in this Christian country. The lurid presentment so powerfully affected her imagination in the silence of the sleeping house that her night-gown became damp with perspiration, and the bedstead shook with each throb of her heart.
>
> The infant's breathing grew more difficult, and the mother's mental tension increased. It was useless to devour the little

thing with kisses; she could stay in bed no longer, and walked feverishly about the room. ...

She lit a candle, and went to a second and a third bed under the wall, where she awoke her young sisters and brothers, all of whom occupied the same room. Pulling out the washing-stand so that she could get behind it, she poured some water from a jug, and made them kneel around, putting their hands together with fingers exactly vertical. While the children, scarcely awake, awestricken at her manner, their eyes growing larger and larger, remained in this position, she took the baby from her bed – a child's child – so immature as scarce to seem a sufficient personality to endow its producer with the maternal title. Tess then stood erect with the infant on her arm beside the basin, the next sister held the Prayer-Book open before her, as the clerk at church held it before the parson; and thus the girl set about baptizing her child. ...

The little ones kneeling round, their sleepy eyes blinking and red, awaited her preparations full of a suspended wonder which their physical heaviness at that hour would not allow to become active.

The most impressed of them said:

'Be you really going to christen him, Tess?'

The girl-mother replied in a grave affirmative.

'What's his name going to be?'

She had not thought of that, but a name suggested by a phrase in the book of Genesis came into her head as she proceeded with the baptismal service, and now she pronounced it:

'Sorrow, I baptize thee in the name of the Father, and of the Son, and of the Holy Ghost.'

She sprinkled the water, and there was silence.

'Say "Amen," children.'

The tiny voices piped in obedient response 'Amen!'

Tess went on:

'We receive this child' – and so forth – 'and do sign him with the sign of the Cross.'

Here she dipped her hand into the basin, and fervently drew an immense cross upon the baby with her forefinger, continuing with the customary sentences as to his manfully fighting against sin, the world, and the devil, and being a faithful soldier and servant unto his life's end. She duly went on with the Lord's Prayer, the children lisping it after her in a thin gnat-like wail, till, at the conclusion, raising their voices to clerk's pitch, they again piped into the silence, 'Amen!' ...

Poor Sorrow's campaign against sin, the world, and the devil was doomed to be of limited brilliancy – luckily perhaps for himself, considering his beginnings. In the blue of the morning that fragile soldier and servant breathed his last, and when the other children awoke they cried bitterly, and begged Sissy to have another pretty baby.

Thomas Hardy (1840–1928), *Tess of the d'Urbervilles*, chapter XIV.

A glory lost and found

In this passage we have a Christian writer also concerned with problems of the theology of infant baptism. The first speaker, the Solitary, is an idealist embittered by adverse experience. Beginning from the traditional under-standing of baptism as the removal of original sin and the child's transfer to the Church as the 'second ark', which, like Noah's, can save from the consequences of divine wrath (cf. 1 Peter 3:20–22), he goes on to suggest that baptism propounds unrealistically high moral aims. The poet makes a partial answer: high ideals can be an inspiration, even if we know we will always fall short of them. The Solitary remains unconvinced: he accepts the value of communally endorsed rituals, but demurs about the main issue, quoting Milton's Satan ('the lost Angel') for the purposes of his own argument, that consciousness of weakness before the ideal leads only to despair (*Paradise Lost*, I. 157).

'Mark the babe
Not long accustomed to this breathing world ...
A day of solemn ceremonial comes;
When they, who for this minor hold in trust
Rights that transcend the loftiest heritage
Of mere humanity, present their charge,
For this occasion daintily adorned,
At the baptismal font. And when the pure
And consecrating element hath cleansed
The original stain, the child is there received
Into the second ark, Christ's church, with trust
That he, from wrath redeemed, therein shall float
Over the billows of this troublesome world
To the fair land of everlasting life.
Corrupt affections, covetous desires,
Are all renounced; high as the thought of man
Can carry virtue, virtue is professed;
A dedication made, a promise given
For due provision to control and guide,
And unremitting progress to ensure

In holiness and truth.'
        'You cannot blame,'
Here interposing fervently I said,
'Rites which attest that Man by nature lies
Bedded for good and evil in a gulf
Fearfully low; nor will your judgment scorn
Those services, whereby attempt is made
To lift the creature toward that eminence
On which, now fallen, erewhile in majesty
He stood; or if not so, whose top serene
At least he feels 'tis given him to descry;
Not without aspirations, evermore
Returning, and injunctions from within
Doubt to cast off and weariness; in trust
That what the soul perceives, if glory lost,
May be, through pains and persevering hope,
Recovered; or, if hitherto unknown,
Lies within reach, and one day shall be gained.'

    'I blame them not,' he calmly answered – 'no;
The outward ritual and established forms
With which communities of men invest
These inward feelings, and the aspiring vows
To which the lips give public utterance
Are both a natural process; and by me
Shall pass uncensured; though the issue prove,
Bringing from age to age its own reproach,
Incongruous, impotent, and blank. – But, oh!
If to be weak is to be wretched – miserable,
As the lost Angel by a human voice
Hath mournfully pronounced, then, in my mind,
Far better not to move at all than move
By impulse sent from such illusive power.'

William Wordsworth (1770–1850), from *The Excursion*,
Book V.

With Jesus' mark impressed

So successful was *The Christian Year* of 1827 that Keble was elected
Professor of Poetry at Oxford in 1831. His poetry's concern for the sacra-
mental life of the Church was to be reflected in the Oxford Movement, the
Catholic reform group whose origins Newman traced to a sermon of

Keble's. Certainly, in this poem Keble makes rich use of symbolism drawn from both the Bible and liturgy, all intended to reinforce the positive character which Wordsworth's Solitary so doubted. The hovering dove reminds us of Christ's own baptism (as in Milton). The next verse alludes to the water and blood which flowed from Christ's side at the Crucifixion (though Keble's use of the image is rather different from Herbert's); while the last verse takes up (as did Coleridge) Paul's image of us as adopted children alongside Christ as God's Son. Then, from the liturgy comes the signing of the brow with the cross, and the reference to the child as a 'young soldier'. In the words of the Book of Common Prayer: 'We receive this child into the congregation of Christ's flock, and do sign him with the sign of the cross, in token that hereafter he shall ... manfully fight under his banner ... and continue Christ's faithful soldier and servant unto his life's end.'

> Where is it mothers learn their love? –
> In every Church a fountain springs
> O'er which th' eternal Dove
> Hovers on softest wings.
>
> What sparkles in that lucid flood
> Is water, by gross mortals eyed:
> But seen by Faith, 'tis blood
> Out of a dear Friend's side....
>
> Blest eyes, that see the smiling gleam
> Upon the slumbering features glow,
> When the life-giving stream
> Touches the tender brow!
>
> Or when the holy cross is signed,
> And the young soldier duly sworn
> With true and fearless mind
> To serve the Virgin-born.
>
> But happiest ye, who sealed and blest
> Back to your arms your treasure take,
> With Jesus' mark impressed
> To nurse for Jesus' sake: ...
>
> O tender gem, and full of Heaven!
> Not in the twilight stars on high,
> Not in moist flowers at even
> See we our God so high.

Sweet one, make haste and know Him too,
Thine own adopting Father love,
That like thine earliest dew
Thy dying sweets may prove.

John Keble (1792–1866), 'Holy Baptism' from *The Christian Year*.

Flowing with the current

Keble writes with a rich and traditional range of symbolic reference. The approach of Flannery O'Connor is simpler, and less dependent on traditions of interpretation. It would be easy to read the bitter humour of her stories as a Catholic satire of Evangelical Christianity in the deep south of the United States; but almost always, as here, there is an underlying religious point. Superficially, this tragicomic story is of a young boy (Bevel), whose uncaring, alcoholic parents have left him in the charge of a child-minder for the day. She takes him to an open-air preachment at which he is baptized. Returning next day to perform the rite more effectively himself, he is drowned in the river. He returns because the preacher had promised that 'you can lay your pain in that River and get rid of it . . . and watch it move away toward the Kingdom of Christ'. The child flowing with the current thus symbolizes what baptism does indeed promise: resurrection and new life. The contrast between a secular reading of what happened and a spiritual is heightened by Mr Paradise's attempts to save him. A scoffer at the earlier baptism, it is he who is now 'empty-handed, staring with his dull eyes'.

By the time Bevel came to the field speckled with purple weeds, he was dusty and sweating and he crossed it at a trot to get into the woods as fast as he could. Once inside, he wandered from tree to tree, trying to find the path they had taken yesterday. Finally he found a line worn in the pine needles and followed it until he saw the steep trail twisting down through the trees.

Mr Paradise had left his automobile back some way on the road and had walked to the place where he was accustomed to sit almost every day, holding an unbaited fish-line in the water while he stared at the river passing in front of him. Anyone looking at him from a distance would have seen an old boulder half hidden in the bushes.

Bevel didn't see him at all. He only saw the river, shimmering reddish yellow, and bounded into it with his shoes and his coat on and took a gulp. He swallowed some and spit the rest out and then he stood there in water up to his chest and looked around him. The sky was a clear pale blue, all in one piece – except for the hole the sun made – and fringed around the bottom with treetops. His coat floated to the surface and surrounded him like a strange gay lily pad and he stood grinning in the sun. He intended not to fool with preachers any more but to Baptize himself and to keep on going this time until he found the Kingdom of Christ in the river. He didn't mean to waste any more time. He put his head under the water at once and pushed forward.

In a second he began to gasp and sputter and his head reappeared on the surface; he started under again and the same thing happened. The river wouldn't have him. He tried again and came up, choking. This was the way it had been when the preacher held him under – he had had to fight with something that pushed him back in the face. He stopped and thought suddenly: it's another joke, it's just another joke! He thought how far he had come for nothing and he began to hit and splash and kick the filthy river. His feet were already treading on nothing. He gave one low cry of pain and indignation. Then he heard a shout and turned his head and saw something like a giant pig bounding after him, shaking a red and white club and shouting. He plunged under once and this time, the waiting current caught him like a long gentle hand and pulled him swiftly forward and down. For an instant he was overcome with surprise; then since he was moving quickly and knew that he was getting somewhere, all his fury and his fear left him.

Mr Paradise's head appeared from time to time on the surface of the water. Finally, far downstream, the old man rose like some ancient water monster and stood empty-handed, staring with his dull eyes as far down the river line as he could see.

Flannery O'Connor (1925–64), from 'The River' from *A Good Man Is Hard to Find*.

Baptism in blood

Born in New York of Presbyterian parents, Melville wrestled throughout his life with religious themes. In particular he objected to what he saw as orthodoxy's failure to treat the reality of evil with sufficient seriousness. Many have seen in the hero of the posthumous *Billy Budd* a Christ-like figure destroyed by evil. In his most famous novel, *Moby Dick*, innocent nature (a white whale) is pursued by the tragically obsessed Captain Ahab. The diabolical baptism of the weapon intended for use in the whale's destruction symbolizes the reversal of Christian baptism: whereas in Flannery O'Connor's story literal death images release into spiritual life, here the intention of a literal death for the whale confirms Ahab in the spiritual death of his obsession.

Perth was about to begin welding the twelve into one, when Ahab stayed his hand, and said he would weld his own iron. As, then, with regular, gasping hems, he hammered on the anvil, Perth passing to him the glowing rods, one after the other, and the hard pressed forge shooting up its intense straight flame, the Parsee passed silently, and bowing over his head towards the fire, seemed invoking some curse or some blessing on the toil. But, as Ahab looked up, he slid aside.

'What's that bunch of lucifers dodging about there for?' muttered Stubb, looking on from the forecastle. 'That Parsee smells fire like a fusee; and smells of it himself, like a hot musket's powder-pan.'

At last the shank, in one complete rod, received its final heat; and as Perth, to temper it, plunged it all hissing into the cask of water near by, the scalding steam shot up into Ahab's bent face.

'Would'st thou brand me, Perth?' wincing for a moment with the pain; 'have I been but forging my own branding-iron, then?'

'Pray God, not that; yet I fear something, Captain Ahab. Is not this harpoon for the White Whale?'

'For the white fiend! But now for the barbs; thou must make them thyself, man. Here are my razors – the best of steel; here, and make the barbs sharp as the needle-sleet of the Icy Sea.'

For a moment, the old blacksmith eyed the razors as though he would fain not use them.

'Take them, man, I have no need for them; for I now neither shave, sup, nor pray till – but here – to work!'

Fashioned at last into an arrowy shape, and welded by Perth to the shank, the steel soon pointed the end of the iron; and as the blacksmith was about giving the barbs their final heat, prior to tempering them, he cried to Ahab to place the water-cask near.

'No, no – no water for that; I want it of the true death-temper. Ahoy, there! Tashtego, Queequeg, Daggoo! What say ye, pagans! Will ye give me as much blood as will cover this barb?' holding it high up. A cluster of dark nods replied, Yes. Three punctures were made in the heathen flesh, and the White Whale's barbs were then tempered.

'Ego non baptizo te in nomine patris, sed in nomine diaboli!'

deliriously howled Ahab, as the malignant iron scorchingly
devoured the baptismal blood.

Herman Melville (1819–91), Moby Dick, chapter 113.

Burning liquors

With this poem we return to the more complex use of symbolism that Keble
favoured. Vaughan quotes as his inspiration the contrast John the Baptist
drew between his own baptism and that of Jesus: 'I indeed baptize you with
water unto repentance, but he … shall baptize you with the Holy Spirit and
with fire' (Matt 3:11). Though greatly influenced by Herbert ('whose holy
life and verse gained many pious converts, of whom I am the least'),
Vaughan's poetry displays a livelier sense of the pervasive presence of God
in the natural world, and in this case the verse generates a thought-
provoking combination of these two natural images for the work of the Holy
Spirit: water and fire. The original context is commonly taken to imply the
fire of judgement, but Vaughan, perhaps drawing upon the 'tongues of fire'
at Pentecost, uses the two images as mutual reinforcement, to suggest
animation and life. He observes how, like the shimmering light of the stars
in the blackness of the night sky, the Holy Spirit, first bestowed at baptism,
can transform our indifference and lethargy to the 'quickness' of a more
intense life.

When to my eyes
(Whilst deep sleep others catches)
Thine host of spies,
The stars, shine in their watches,
I do survey
Each busy ray,
And how they work, and wind,
And wish each beam
My soul doth stream
With the like ardour shined.
What emanations,
Quick vibrations,
And bright stirs are there!
What thin ejections,
Cold affections,
And slow motions here!

Thy heavens (some say)
Are a fiery-liquid light,
Which, mingling aye,
Streams and flames thus to the sight.

Come then, my God!
Shine on this blood
And water in one beam,
    And thou shalt see
    Kindled by thee
Both liquors burn and stream.
    O what bright quickness,
    Active brightness,
And celestial flows
    Will follow after
    On that water
Which thy Spirit blows!

Henry Vaughan (1622–95), 'Midnight'.

CONFIRMED IN FAITH

Introduction

In the New Testament, with Christianity still largely a religion of recent converts, inevitably the focus is on the baptism of adults. Even so, twice (Acts 8:14–18; 19:5–6) a two-stage process is indicated, with the Holy Spirit given by the apostles through a laying on of hands subsequent to baptism. It was this two-stage process which was to become the norm in the Catholic West, while the Orthodox East maintained a single rite even though they too moved towards infant baptism as the norm. The decisive factor for the West was the refusal of its bishops to delegate the 'confirming' of the baptism to the parish clergy. The resultant need to wait until the bishop was available, combined with arguments about the necessity for the child to appropriate for itself the promises made at baptism, resulted in present practice in the Roman and Anglican churches. The latter still in many areas follows medieval practice in making admission to communion consequent on confirmation, whereas in modern Roman Catholicism (and in some parts of the Anglican Communion) first communion often precedes confirmation. In the West, though oil is sometimes also used, the primary sacramental focus lies with the bishop laying his hands upon the confirmand, whereas in the East it is the priest's anointing with oil that is seen as central.

But, whatever the differences of detail, the most obvious contrast between West and East has been the way in which in the West the rite has come to be seen as the taking of full responsibility for promises originally made on one's behalf at baptism. It thus marks the transition to full membership of the Christian community. But at what age should this take place? The medieval tradition opted for the age of reason, which it identified as seven; Anglican practice has often placed it later, nearer puberty; while in non-episcopal churches the equivalent – the elders extending the right hand of fellowship – is reserved for early adulthood.

In what follows the earlier passages focus upon the transitional character of the rite, and the anxieties which flow from this. For Wordsworth confirmation marks the sun setting upon childhood, but youthful enthusiasm to press on to the next stage is often tempered not only by priestly anxieties (Hopkins) but also by the rite failing to meet the young person's expectations (White). Traditionally, the transition has been marked by symbolism: for girls marriage to Christ (Levertov, Dickinson); for boys soldiering (Cather, Keble). But the stereotyping of gender roles, combined with the desire to disengage the rite from the confusing associations of growing sexual awareness (Lewis), have meant that, with the possible exception of confession, it is the sacrament currently most under reconsideration.

Their own lips speak

Wordsworth wrote over a hundred 'Ecclesiastical Sonnets'. Most have as their theme the history of the Church in England, but this sonnet is one of three dedicated to the theme of confirmation. It captures with admirable conciseness the rite as a conscious 'confirming' of the vows made on one's behalf at baptism, whereby that earlier covenant is 'sealed' (2 Cor 1:20–22). That this is entry into a church in continuity with the New Testament Wordsworth stresses with his description of the bishop's hand as 'apostolic'.

> The young ones gathered in from hill and dale,
> With holiday delight on every brow:
> 'Tis past away; far other thoughts prevail;
> For they are taking the baptismal vow
> Upon their conscious selves; their own lips speak
> The solemn promise. Strongest sinews fail,
> And many a blooming, many a lovely, cheek
> Under the holy fear of God turns pale;
> While on each head his lawn-robed servant lays
> An apostolic hand, and with prayer seals
> The Covenant. The Omnipotent will raise
> Their feeble souls; and bear with *his* regrets,
> Who, looking round the fair assemblage, feels
> That ere the sun goes down their childhood sets.
>
> William Wordsworth (1770–1850), 'Confirmation' from
> *Ecclesiastical Sonnets.*

Twice blessed

Confirmation ought only to be administered once. Sometimes, however, youthful enthusiasm to prove one's new-found adult identity can gain the upper hand, even in someone with as saintly a reputation as Nicholas Ferrar, close friend of George Herbert, and founder of the community at Little Gidding which T. S. Eliot so admired. In his biography of his brother, John

Ferrar tells how Nicholas presented himself a second time for confirmation by Richard Bancroft, the then Bishop of London, in 1598. When challenged by his schoolmaster, he cheerfully replied: 'I did it because it was a good thing to have the bishop's prayers and blessing twice, and I have got it.' In this extract Francis Kilvert tells of a more unusual twist to someone thus 'twice blessed', the bishop himself taking a hand.

In Hadley's shop I met Dewing who told me of a most extraordinary misfortune that befell Pope the curate of Cusop yesterday at the Whitney Confirmation. He had one candidate Miss Stokes a farmer's daughter and they went together by train. Pope went in a cutaway coat very short, with his dog, and took no gown. The train was very late. He came very late into church and sat down on a bench with the girl cheek by jowl. When it came to his turn to present his candidate he was told by the Rector (Henry Dew) or someone in authority to explain why he came so late. The Bishop of Hereford (Atlay) has a new fashion of confirming only two persons at a time, kneeling at the rails. The Bishop had marked two young people come in very late and when they came up to the rails he thought from Pope's youthful appearance and from his having no gown that he was a young farmer candidate and brother of the girl. He spoke to them severely and told them to come on and kneel down for they were extremely late. Pope tried to explain that he was a clergyman and that the girl was his candidate but the Bishop was overbearing and imperious and either did not hear or did not attend, seeming to think he was dealing with a refractory ill-conditioned youth. 'I know, I know,' he said. 'Come at once, kneel down, kneel down.' Poor Pope resisted a long time and had a long battle with the Bishop, but at last unhappily he was overborne in the struggle, lost his head, gave way, knelt down and was *confirmed* there and then, and no one seems to have interfered to save him, though Mr Palmer of Eardisley and others were sitting close by and the whole Church was in a titter. It is a most unfortunate thing and will never be forgotten and it will be unhappily a joke against Pope all his life. The Bishop was told of his mistake afterwards and apologized to Pope, though rather shortly and cavalierly. He said, what was quite true, that Pope ought to have come in his gown. But there was a little fault on all sides for if the Bishop had been a little less hasty, rough and overbearing in his manner things might have been explained, and the bystanding clergy were certainly very much to blame for

not stepping forward and preventing such a farce. I fear poor
Pope will be very much vexed, hurt and dispirited about it.

Francis Kilvert, Diary, April Eve, 1870.

Youthful promise in regimental red

Partly because of its stronger eucharistic tradition, and partly because in
modern practice confirmation does not always precede first communion, in
much Roman Catholic thinking it is first communion rather than confirmation which is seen as decisively marking the transition to mature
responsibilities of Christian adulthood. Here, moved by the awesome
responsibility of giving a first communion and by the eagerness and purity of
the communicant, Hopkins, the young Jesuit priest, asks that the boy be
protected from evil. Despite fears that he may lapse from his present
innocence, Hopkins entrusts him to Christ's protection with a confidence
which is at once defiant and tentative. (The 'sendings' of divine grace come
in a 'leaf-light' wafer for which Hopkins uses the mystery-evoking medieval
term, the 'housel'.)

A bugler boy from barrack (it is over the hill
There) – boy bugler, born, he tells me, of Irish
   Mother to an English sire (he
Shares their best gifts surely, fall how things will),

This very very day came down to us after a boon he on
My late being there begged of me, overflowing
   Boon in my bestowing,
Came, I say, this day to it – to a First Communion.

Here he knelt then in regimental red.
Forth Christ from cupboard fetched, how fain I of feet
   To his youngster take his treat!
Low-latched in leaf-light housel his too huge godhead.

There! and your sweetest sendings, ah divine,
By it, heavens, befall him! as a heart Christ's darling,
     dauntless;
   Tongue true, vaunt- and tauntless;
Breathing bloom of a chastity in mansex fine.

Frowning and forefending angel-warder
Squander the hell-rook   *disperse*
     ranks sally to molest him;   *(ranks which sally)*
   March, kind comrade, abreast him;
Dress his days to a dexterous and starlight order. . . .

O now well work that sealing sacred ointment!
O for now charms, arms, what bans off bad
   And locks love ever in a lad!
Let me though see no more of him, and not disappointment

Those sweet hopes quell whose least me quickenings lift,
In scarlet or somewhere of some day seeing
   That brow and bead of being,
An our day's God's own Galahad. Though this child's drift

Seems by a divine doom channelled, nor do I cry
Disaster there; but may he not rankle and roam
   In backwheels though bound home? –
That left to the Lord of the Eucharist, I here lie by;

Recorded only, I have put my lips on pleas
Would brandle adamantine heaven with   *shake*
      ride and jar, did   *shock and clash*
   Prayer go disregarded:
Forward-like, but however, and   *presumptuous*
      like favourable heaven heard these.   *probably*

Gerard Manley Hopkins (1844–89), from 'The Bugler's First Communion'.

The unlit coal

Wordsworth, Ferrar and Hopkins all spoke of youthful enthusiasm, as 'childhood set' and the rite initiated the young person into full membership of the Christian community. *Frost in May* is an autobiographical novel set in 1908, drawing upon Antonia White's own education in a convent from which, like Nanda in the novel, she was expelled for writing fiction about love. Here too we have youthful enthusiasm, with Nanda getting up at six and reciting the night office prayer (Ps 119:55; 1 Cor 16:22) whenever she wakes. But, as the choir sings in Latin 'O Jesus, for whom I have long sighed, at last I hold you', her only thought is failure: she is an 'unlit coal'. The novel as a whole is critical of Catholicism, which Antonia White rejected for many years, but it later provoked the moving correspondence recorded in *The Hound and the Falcon* that was to lead to her reconversion.

In the summer term that followed her eleventh birthday, Nanda began to prepare for her First Communion. She was in the Senior School now, where life was a sterner, more responsible affair, symbolised by a black serge apron instead of a blue pinafore. She got up for mass every morning at six o'clock and stayed up until nine at night. There were all kinds of new

subjects to study ... music, history, botany, German, mathe-
matics, deportment, and Catholic Apologetics. The old days of
learning the simpler pages of the catechism and the stories of
the saints were succeeded by a study of the knottier points of
dogma ... a study to which she was to devote at least an hour a
day for the next few years. ...

The great day came at last. Every time she woke up during the
night before, which was often, Nanda said, as she had been told
to do:

'Even in the night have I desired thee, Lord. Come, Lord
Jesus, come.'

Everything she put on that morning was new and white. A
white prayer-book and a mother-of-pearl rosary, a gift from
Reverend Mother, lay beside her new veil, and the stiff wreath of
white cotton roses that every First Communicant wore. They
walked into the chapel two by two, pacing slowly up the aisle like
twelve brides, to the sound of soft, lacy music. In front of the
altar were twelve prie-dieu covered with white muslin and
flowers, with a tall candle burning in front of each. At little stools
at the side knelt the children from the Poor School, who were
also making their First Communion. They had no candles, and
their cotton frocks looked shabby.

Nanda tried to fix her attention on the mass, but she could
not. She felt light-headed and empty, unable to pray or even to
think. ...

Nanda was horrified at her own detachment, she tried hard to
concentrate on the great moment ahead of her, but her mind
was blank. In a trance she heard the bell ring for the *Domine non
sum dignus*, and heard the rustle as the others got up to go to the
altar rails. In terror, she thought: 'I haven't made a proper
preparation. I've been distracted the whole time, to-day of all
days. Dare I go up with them?' But almost without knowing, her
body had moved with the rest, and she was kneeling at the rails
with the others, holding the embroidered cloth under her chin.
Under her almost closed eyelids, she could see the pattern of the
altar carpet, and the thin, round hosts, like honesty leaves, in the
ciborium. The priest was opposite her now; she raised her head
and shut her eyes tight. She felt the wafer touch her tongue and
waited for some extraordinary revelation, for death even. But she
felt nothing.

Back at her prie-dieu, she kept her head bowed like the
others. Above the noise in her ears she could hear the choir
singing softly and dreamily:

'Ad quem diu suspiravi,
Jesu tandem habeo.'

Over and over she told herself frantically:

'This is the greatest moment of my life. Our Lord Himself is actually present, in the flesh, inside my body. Why am I so numb and stupid? Why can't I think of anything to say?' She was relieved when the quarter of an hour's thanksgiving was over. As they filed out of the chapel she looked at the faces of the other eleven, to see if they felt as she did. But every face was gay or recollected or content ... With all her efforts, all her devotion, there was something wrong with her. Perhaps a convert could never ring quite true. Perhaps real Catholics were right always to mistrust and despise them a little. For weeks she had been preparing herself, laying stick on stick and coal on coal, and now, at the supreme moment, she had not caught fire. Her First Communion had been a failure.

Antonia White (1899–1979), Frost in May, chapter 4.

Married to Christ

Antonia White described how Nanda and her companions, all dressed in white, 'paced slowly up the aisle like twelve brides'. More than metaphor was involved in that description, since for girls traditionally the way of marking the new identity has been to use veil and white dress to symbolize marriage to Christ. Denise Levertov here builds on that symbolism, talking also of the 'bridal cake'. In ending, however, with the confirmands dressed in 'bloodred velvet', the poem hints – ironically through their spontaneous play – that the responsibilities of adulthood, 'bloodred' like Christ's life, cannot now be far off.

> After the First Communion
> and the banquet of mangoes and
> bridal cake, the young daughters
> of the coffee merchant lay down
> for a long siesta, and their white dresses
> lay beside them in quietness
> and the white veils floated
> in their dreams as the flies buzzed.
> But as the afternoon
> burned to a close they rose
> and ran about the neighborhood
> among the halfbuilt villas

alive, alive, kicking a basketball, wearing
other new dresses, of bloodred velvet.

Denise Levertov (b. 1923), 'Sunday Afternoon'
from *With Eyes At the Back of Our Heads*.

A crowned queen

Despite her Congregationalist background Emily Dickinson draws here
heavily on Catholic imagery, to underline the contrast between involuntary
baptism and the conscious acceptance for oneself of one's new identity in
confirmation. Whereas at baptism a name was 'dropped on my face', now
confirmation suggests larger possibilities, including the taking of a new
name. But, as with White and Levertov, it is with the image of marriage that
Dickinson finds this transition most effectively portrayed. The bridal coro-
net speaks of a new dignity – 'adequate, erect' – which even allows her to
speak of herself (as in the Orthodox marriage service) as a 'queen'.

I'm ceded: I've stopped being theirs.
The name they dropped upon my face
With water, in the country church,
Is finished using now,
And they can put it with my dolls,
My childhood, and the strings of spools
I've finished threading too.

Baptized before without the choice,
But this time consciously, of grace,
Unto supremest name;
Called to my full, the crescent dropped,
Existence's whole arc filled up
With one small diadem.

My second rank – too small the first,
Crowned, crowing on my father's breast,
A half-unconscious queen –
But this time adequate, erect,
With will to choose or to reject,
And I choose just a crown.

Emily Dickinson (1830–86), *c.* 1862.

Life's jig-a-jig

To use the imagery of marriage for confirmation has obvious dangers in that
issues of sexuality and Christian initiation can then easily become confused
in the young person's mind. That is no doubt why, unlike most pagan
initiation rites which were deliberately intended to coincide with puberty,

confirmation was soon fixed much earlier at the age of rationality, and by the late Middle Ages seven had become the norm. Subsequent Anglican practice has often set it later, and some of the perhaps inevitable consequences are recorded below.

> Every boy in the village, without exception and including myself, attended these classes, purely because of the irresistible benefits they entailed, although I cannot remember a single one who after confirmation bothered any more with the Church. A series of ten classes were held and, as we saw it, it was worth putting up with the boredom of nine of them for the top-rate entertainment offered by the tenth, on the subject of sex. In this class Mr Bowles discussed the facts of life with extreme frankness, and we had learned from boys attending the classes of previous years of an interesting demonstration he could be encouraged to give if faced by what he believed to be total incomprehension. For this purpose he kept ready two antique French dolls, and when at our last class there were cries from us of, 'He doesn't understand, sir. Show him your jig-a-jig,' Mr Bowles unlocked and opened a drawer under his birds' egg cabinet and took these out. In the rather solemn and awestruck tone he normally used for reading the lesson in church, he drew our attention to the manner in which they were joined together. After that, a match was put to the combustion chamber of a tiny steam engine fuelled by cotton wool soaked in methylated spirits, to which the dolls were connected, and soon the tiny hips started to bounce, first slowly, then frantically as the engine warmed up, till finally with an ecstatic squeak of steam through a valve it was all over. A brief prayer in which we all joined followed, and our preparation for life was at an end.

> Norman Lewis, *Jackdaw Cake* (1985).

Soldiers of Christ

Just as marriage has commonly been used as the appropriate symbol for girls, so soldiering has been for boys. In this, confirmation develops the baptismal injunction 'to continue Christ's faithful soldier'. In the following extract from Willa Cather's *O Pioneers!*, the story of a frontier farming family set in the Midwest of Cather's own background, the young men ride out to meet the bishop, longing 'for a Jerusalem to deliver'. The bishop's ready acceptance of military imagery ('The Church still has her cavalry') chimes well with one traditional aspect of the confirmation service – the Alapa, the blow he gives to the confirmand's cheek to symbolize the spiritual warfare ahead.

The Church has always held that life is for the living. On Saturday, while half the village of Sainte-Agnes was mourning for Amédée and preparing the funeral black for his burial on Monday, the other half was busy with white dresses and white veils for the great confirmation service to-morrow, when the bishop was to confirm a class of one hundred boys and girls. Father Duchesne divided his time between the living and the dead. All day Saturday the church was a scene of bustling activity, a little hushed by the thought of Amédée. The choir were busy rehearsing a mass of Rossini, which they had studied and practised for this occasion. The women were trimming the altar, the boys and girls were bringing flowers.

On Sunday morning the bishop was to drive overland to Sainte-Agnes from Hanover, and Emil Bergson had been asked to take the place of one of Amédée's cousins in the cavalcade of forty French boys who were to ride across country to meet the bishop's carriage. At six o'clock on Sunday morning the boys met at the church. As they stood holding their horses by the bridle, they talked in low tones of their dead comrade.

When the word was given to mount, the young men rode at a walk out of the village; but once out among the wheatfields in the morning sun, their horses and their own youth got the better of them. A wave of zeal and fiery enthusiasm swept over them. They longed for a Jerusalem to deliver. The thud of their galloping hoofs interrupted many a country breakfast and brought many a woman and child to the door of the farmhouses as they passed. Five miles east of Sainte-Agnes they met the bishop in his open carriage, attended by two priests. Like one man the boys swung off their hats in a broad salute, and bowed their heads as the handsome old man lifted his two fingers in the episcopal blessing. The horsemen closed about the carriage like a guard, and whenever a restless horse broke from control and shot down the road ahead of the body, the bishop laughed and rubbed his plump hands together. 'What fine boys!' he said to his priests. 'The Church still has her cavalry.' ...

When all the pews were full, the old men and boys packed the open space at the back of the church, kneeling on the floor. There was scarcely a family in town that was not represented in the confirmation class, by a cousin, at least. The new communicants, with their clear, reverent faces, were beautiful to look upon as they entered in a body and took the front benches reserved for them. Even before the Mass began, the air was charged with feeling. ...

The confirmation service followed the Mass. When it was over, the congregation thronged about the newly confirmed. The girls, and even the boys, were kissed and embraced and wept over. All the aunts and grandmothers wept with joy.

Willa Cather (1873–1947), *O Pioneers!*, chapter 6.

The desert army

Keble, like Cather, uses military imagery. The Dove of the Holy Spirit descending on the confirmand is compared to the cloud which guided the children of Israel by day in their flight through the wilderness to the Promised Land (Exod 13:17–22). Just as they were equipped for battle (v. 18), so too must the new Christians be. Like Hopkins, Keble looks towards the difficulties that lie ahead, praying that the awesome moment of confirmation will remain in the memory to guard and guide. But, like that ancient desert army, the confirmands cannot fail provided they look to the 'sheltering rock' whose water never runs dry (Num 20:2–13; 1 Cor 10:4).

> The shadow of th' Almighty's cloud
>   Calm on the tents of Israel lay,
> While drooping paused twelve banners proud,
>   Till He arise and lead the way.
>
> Then to the desert breeze unrolled,
>   Cheerly the waving pennons fly,
> Lion or eagle – each bright fold
>   A lodestar to a warrior's eye.
>
> So should Thy champions, ere the strife,
>   By holy lands o'ershadowed kneel,
> So, fearless for their charmèd life,
>   Bear, to the end, Thy Spirit's seal.
>
> Steady and pure as stars that beam
>   In middle heaven, all mist above,
> Seen deepest in the frozen stream: –
>   Such is their high courageous love.
>
> And soft as pure, and warm as bright,
>   They brood upon life's peaceful hour,
> As if the Dove that guides their flight
>   Shook from her plumes a downy shower.

Spirit of might and sweetness too!
   Now leading on the wars of God,
Now to green isles of shade and dew
   Turning the waste Thy people trod;

Draw, Holy Ghost, Thy seven-fold veil
   Between us and the fires of youth;
Breathe, Holy Ghost, Thy freshening gale,
   Our fevered brow in age to soothe.

And oft as sin and sorrow tire,
   The hallowed hour do Thou renew,
When beckoned up the awful choir
   By pastoral hands, toward Thee we drew;

When trembling at the sacred rail
   We hid our eyes and held our breath,
Felt Thee how strong, our hearts how frail,
   And longed to own Thee to the death.

For ever on our souls be traced
   That blessing dear, that dove-like hand,
A sheltering rock in Memory's waste,
   O'er-shadowing all the weary land.

     John Keble (1792–1866), 'Confirmation' from *The Christian*
                                              Year.

BREAD OF HEAVEN

Introduction

Almost all Christians are agreed on the centrality of the eucharist to the Church's life, and in this they reflect the witness of the New Testament. In very early times, as we see from Paul, it became the central act of Christian worship (1 Cor 11:17–34); three of the Gospels record its institution at the Last Supper (Matt 26:26–28; Mark 14:22–24; Luke 22:17–20), while the fourth offers us an extended reflection on the significance of partaking in Christ's flesh and blood (John 6:32–58). Since 'eucharist' is now the most commonly used term, that is the one we adopt, but the various terms all tell us something about this particular sacrament. Thus, 'the Lord's Supper' continues to recall its original setting in the context of a meal; 'eucharist' (the Greek for 'thanksgiving') alludes both to Jesus's original prayer of thankfulness over the bread and wine and to the believer's present thankfulness for what God has done in Christ (the prayer of consecration is itself sometimes called 'the thanksgiving'); 'mass' emphasizes the continuity of the tradition, derived as it is from the concluding words of the Latin rite – *Ite; missa est* (Go; you have been sent forth); while 'Holy Communion' speaks of the union effected by the sacrament between Christ and the believer, and through Christ among the believers themselves.

As with baptism a tension may be observed between a backward- and a forward-looking emphasis. Is the primary purpose to recall Christ's sacrificial death upon the cross ('do this in remembrance of me'), and the promise of release from sin which it brought, or should the primary focus instead be on Christ working in the here and now to transform us ('I am the bread of life . . . he who eats this bread will live for ever')? In the first group of extracts release from sin is to the fore, and in the case of Samuel Johnson the connection with baptism is made quite explicit. But this is not an exclusively Protestant emphasis, as the two converts, Meynell and Eliot (in his case to Anglo-Catholicism), illustrate. With Lancelot Andrewes we move to the theme of transformation. Here likewise we find an idea shared across denominational boundaries, as well as adaptations of the symbolism to a more secular purpose (Dylan Thomas, Wallace Stevens).

However, with the issue of the precise nature of Christ's presence in the consecrated bread and wine, no such unanimity can be claimed. For some a well-known verse attributed to Queen Elizabeth I will suffice: 'Christ was the word who spake it, / Christ took the bread and brake it, / And what his word doth make it, / That I believe and take it.' For others the doctrine of transubstantiation (Crashaw, Southwell, Constable) will be the only proper culmination of a sacramental tradition that sees God operating everywhere through the medium of the physical; while yet others will delight in the satirical protests of Jonathan Swift, or the purely spiritual interpretation given by Edward Taylor.

But, however conceived, even when there is great longing for union with Christ through the sacrament this is not always achieved, and so the next extracts look at the issue of failure and its possible resolution. Does the problem lie with the intellect (Tolstoy), or with the emotions (Hill)? Yet again, might it lie in discovering a general pattern of divine action through matter or the physical as God's instrument? This is often given as a justification for ritual. So the section ends with a selection of contrasting views, from the uncompromising hostility of Emerson to the unqualified enthusiasm of Betjeman.

The covenant renewed

Samuel Johnson was one of the major intellectual figures of the eighteenth century. A devout Anglican layman, in this extract from one of his sermons, he connects baptism and eucharist through the original meaning of the Latin word *sacramentum*, 'oath'. Holy Communion provides an opportunity to renew the covenant of allegiance to Christ which others undertook on our behalf at baptism and which we have broken through sin. That backward-looking emphasis is given further impetus when, as here, the primary element in the eucharist is seen as commemoration and appropriation of the benefits of Christ's death. This plain doctrinal statement, with its calm discussion of covenant-breaking by sin, contrasts with the many diary entries which reveal Johnson's acute sensitivity to his own sinfulness and the consequent intensity of feeling with which he approached taking communion. For example, after recording days of fasting and concentrated preparation: 'Shall I ever receive the Sacrament with tranquillity? Surely the time will come' (Easter Day, 15 April 1770).

> By commemorating the death of Christ, as the Redeemer of the world, we confess our belief in him; for why else should we perform so solemn a rite in commemoration of him? To confess our belief in him, is to declare ourselves his followers. We enter into an obligation to perform those conditions upon which he has admitted us to follow him, and to practise all the duties of that religion which he has taught us.

This is implied in the word sacrament, which, being originally used to signify an oath of fidelity taken by the soldiers to their leaders, is now made use of by the church, to import a solemn vow, of unshaken adherence to the faith of Christ.

Thus the sacrament is a kind of repetition of baptism, the means whereby we are readmitted into the communion of the church of Christ, when we have, by sin, been separated from it; for every sin, and much more any habit or course of sin long continued, is, according to the different degrees of guilt, an apostasy or defection from our Saviour; as it is a breach of those conditions upon which we became his followers; and he that breaks the condition of a covenant, dissolves it on his side. Having therefore broken the covenant between us and our Redeemer, we lose the benefits of his death; nor can we have any hopes of obtaining them, while we remain in this state of separation from him.

But vain had been the sufferings of our Saviour, had there not been left means of reconciliation to him; since every man falls away from him occasionally, by sins of negligence at least, and perhaps, by known, deliberate, premeditated offences. So that some method of renewing the covenant between God and man was necessary; and for this purpose this sacrament was instituted; which is therefore a renewal of our broken vows, a re-entrance into the society of the church, and the act, by which we are restored to the benefits of our Saviour's death, upon performance of the terms prescribed by him.

So that this sacrament is a solemn ratification of a covenant renewed; by which, after having alienated ourselves from Christ by sin, we are restored, upon our repentance and reformation, to pardon and favour, and the certain hopes of everlasting life.

Samuel Johnson (1709–84), Sermon on 1 Corinthians 11:28.

Guilt's plea

The poet William Cowper suffered bouts of depression throughout his life in which he was supported by a retired Evangelical clergyman, Morley Unwin, and after Unwin's death by his wife Mary. It was she who nursed Cowper back to health in 1776 when he found himself overwhelmed by intellectual and emotional pressures from their new friend, the Calvinist former slave-owner John Newton, and he was able to make a number of fine contributions to the new hymn-book Newton produced in 1779, *Olney Hymns*. Here, the first two stanzas illustrate the freedom of the poet to go beyond the conventions of particular denominational orthodoxies: Jesus is unequivocally identified with the 'vine' (John 15:1–7) and the bread. However, in the second half of the poem Johnson's primary focus recurs: the Lord's table brings refreshment to those, like the poet, weighed down by guilt and care.

> This is the feast of heav'nly wine,
>   And GOD invites to sup;
> The juices of the living vine
>   Were pressed, to fill the cup.
>
> Oh, bless the Saviour, ye that eat,
>   With royal dainties fed;
> Not heav'n affords a costlier treat,
>   For JESUS is the bread!
>
> The vile, the lost, he calls to them,
>   Ye trembling souls appear!
> The righteous, in their own esteem,
>   Have no acceptance here.
>
> Approach ye poor, nor dare refuse
>   The banquet spread for you;
> Dear Saviour, this is welcome news,
>   Then I may venture too.
>
> If guilt and sin afford a plea,
>   And may obtain a place;
> Surely the LORD will welcome me,
>   And I shall see his face!
>
> William Cowper (1731–1800), 'Welcome
> to the Table' from *Olney Hymns*.

The hunted prey

It would be wrong, however, to suppose that the eucharist bringing release from sin is a purely Protestant notion. In the following poem, Alice Meynell starts by accepting the accusation of a critic of the Church, that Christians hunt down Christ by sin, thoughtlessness, even sheer comfortable complacency. It remains, none the less, the case that it is the hunted prey who feeds the believer, and so by implication also offers release from sin.

> 'We have hunted down Jesus Christ'
>
> Yes, from the ingrate heart, the street
> Of garrulous tongue, the warm retreat
>   Within the village and the town;
>   Not from the lands where ripen brown
> A thousand thousand hills of wheat;

Not from the long Burgundian line,
The Southward, sunward range of vine.
Hunted, He never will escape
The flesh, the blood, the sheaf, the grape,
That feed His man – the bread, the wine.

Alice Meynell (1847–1922), 'The Fugitive'.

The ungrateful guest

How is 'the ingrate heart' of Alice Meynell's poem to respond? Though,
Herbert observes, we cannot look on Christ for shame, yet all we need recall
is that it is he who made the eyes that turn away, he who took flesh and
thereby 'bore the blame'. The sacramental participation of God in the world
thus provides the answer, and so we can with confidence 'sit down' and
'taste [his] meat' (Luke 12:37).

Love bade me welcome, yet my soul drew back,
        Guilty of dust and sin.
But quick-eyed Love, observing me grow slack
        From my first entrance in,
Drew nearer to me, sweetly questioning,
        If I lacked any thing.

A guest, I answered, worthy to be here:
        Love said, You shall be he.
I the unkind, ungrateful? Ah my dear,
        I cannot look on thee.
Love took my hand, and smiling did reply,
        Who made the eyes but I?

Truth Lord, but I have marred them: let my shame
        Go where it doth deserve.
And know you not, says Love, who bore the blame?
        My dear, then I will serve.
You must sit down, says Love, and taste my meat:
        So I did sit and eat.

George Herbert (1593–1633), 'Love (III)'.

Our only health disease

T. S. Eliot was converted to Christianity in 1927. That the form of his piety
was Anglo-Catholic is well illustrated by this lyric from *Four Quartets*. He
sees our cure in physical terms: the 'fleshly' character of the eucharist is

strongly emphasized. Christ becomes the wounded surgeon attempting to
heal us, the Church is our nurse, the world our hospital, and the eucharistic
elements hospital food. Eliot claims, paradoxically, that spiritual sickness is
a form of health: if we acknowledge it fully, we come to understand better
Christ's compassion for us and our ultimate dependence upon God's grace,
which works through the cares of this world, and not despite them. That is
why, following the Prayer Book, he can talk of God's grace 'preventing (i.e.
'going before') us everywhere' (optional prayer in the Communion service,
and Collect for 17th Sunday after Trinity).

> The wounded surgeon plies the steel
> That questions the distempered part;
> Beneath the bleeding hands we feel
> The sharp compassion of the healer's art
> Resolving the enigma of the fever chart.
>
> Our only health is the disease
> If we obey the dying nurse
> Whose constant care is not to please
> But to remind of our, and Adam's curse,
> And that, to be restored, our sickness must grow worse.
>
> The whole earth is our hospital
> Endowed by the ruined millionaire,
> Wherein, if we do well, we shall
> Die of the absolute paternal care
> That will not leave us, but prevents us everywhere.
>
> The chill ascends from feet to knees,
> The fever sings in mental wires.
> If to be warmed, then I must freeze
> And quake in frigid purgatorial fires
> Of which the flame is roses, and the smoke is briars.
>
> The dripping blood our only drink,
> The bloody flesh our only food:
> In spite of which we like to think
> That we are sound, substantial flesh and blood –
> Again, in spite of that, we call this Friday good.
>
> T. S. Eliot (1888–1965), *East Coker*, IV, from *Four Quartets*.

The house of bread

With this extract the theme of transformation moves to centre stage.
Lancelot Andrewes was one of the great preachers of the seventeenth
century. Already Dean of Westminster when James I became king, he was

advanced in turn to the bishoprics of Chichester, Ely and Winchester. Andrewes' style, which on the page may present difficulties because its grammar is by modern standards elliptical, is that of a preacher writing for the speaking voice. His prose was greatly admired by T. S. Eliot, whose 'Journey of the Magi' takes as its starting point one of Andrewes' sermons. Here Andrewes plays on the etymology of Bethlehem as the town of Jesus's birth, to suggest that our lives' pilgrimage is to 'the house of bread'. He draws an analogy between the processes by which bread and wine are made and the sufferings of Christ, and then between the Church and Bethlehem. There, like corn being made into bread, we too will be transformed – not merely to the state of Adam and Eve in Paradise, but carried beyond to share with Christ in the life of heaven.

> He is not a good guide who cannot lead us where we may be purveyed of necessary food for our relief. It is all one, to perish out of the way, by error; and to perish in the way, by want of needful refreshing. St Matthew therefore, to make Him a complete guide, by way of supply adds *qui pascet* [who shall feed]; such a One as shall lead 'as a shepherd doth his flock'; not lead them the way only, but lead them also to good green pasture beside the waters of comfort, see they want nothing.
>
> The name of the place he was born in seems to favour this most. *Beth* is a house; *lehem* is bread; and *Ephratah* is plenty – 'bread-plenty'. Bethlehem then, sure, a fit place for *qui pascet* to be born in; and *qui pascet* a fit person to be born in Bethlehem. Never take Him without bread: His house is the house of bread, inasmuch as He Himself is bread; that, in the house or out of it, wheresoever He is, there is Bethlehem. There can no bread want. ...
>
> Christ is Himself the 'true Manna'; Christ, the spiritual rock. Whom He leads, He feeds; carries Bethlehem about Him. Plain, by ordaining of His last sacrament, as the means to re-establish our hearts with grace, and to repair the decay of our spiritual strength; even His own flesh, the bread of life; and His own blood, the cup of salvation. Bread, made of Himself, the true wheat corn. Wine, made of Himself, the true vine. Went under the sickle, flail, millstone, and oven, even to be made this bread; trod, or was trodden, in the winepress alone, to be made this cup for us. And in this respect it may well be said Bethlehem was never Bethlehem right, had never the name truly, till this day, this birth, this bread was born and brought forth there. Before it was the house of bread, but of the bread that perisheth; but then, of the bread that endureth to everlasting life. ...

We speak of going thither [to Bethlehem]. That we may, even locally, do, and never go out of this room, inasmuch as here is to be had the true bread of life that came down from heaven. Which is His flesh, this day born, which he gave for the life of the world, called by Him so, the true bread, the bread of heaven, the bread of life: and where that bread is, there is Bethlehem ever. Even it may be said, and said truly, the Church, in this sense, is very Bethlehem no less than the town itself. For that the town itself never had the name rightly all the while there was but bread made there, bread, the bread of men. Not till this bread was born there, which is *panis angelorum* as the psalm calleth it [78:25], 'and man did eat angels' food'. Then, and never till then, was it Bethlehem; and that is, in the Church, as truly as ever in it. There shall ever be this day a Bethlehem to go to, a house wherein there is bread, and this bread. And shall there be Bethlehem, and so near us, and we not go to it? Or shall we go to it, the house of bread, this bread, and come away without it? Shall we forsake our guide leading us to a place so much to our benefit?

To end: leading He feeds us, and feeding He leads us, till He bring us – whither? Even back again to where we were at the beginning; and at the beginning we were in Paradise. That our beginning shall be our end. Thither He will bring us; nay, to a better state than so; to that whereunto even from Paradise we should have been translated, to the state of eternity, to the joys and joyful days there; even to glory, joy, and bliss eternal.

Lancelot Andrewes (1555–1626), Christmas Day Sermon, 1615, on Micah 6:2.

Singing, springing corn

Written in 1911, *The Everlasting Mercy* is John Masefield's most famous narrative poem. It tells of the conversion of Saul Kane, who in the pub at closing time taunts the Quaker Miss Bourne with his lewd songs once too often. Something snaps, and, having spent the night wandering in penitent mood, at dawn he catches sight of a plough team at work, and immediately draws the message of transformation implicit in 'the young green corn', 'the golden harvest's yield' and 'the holy bread' which it becomes. The image is the same as Andrewes', but very differently expressed.

> Slow up the hill the plough team plod,
> Old Callow at the task of God,
> Helped by man's wit, helped by the brute
> Turning a stubborn clay to fruit,
> His eyes for ever on some sign

To help him plough a perfect line.
At top of rise the plough team stopped,
The fore-horse bent his head and cropped.
Then the chains chack, the brasses jingle,
The lean reins gather through the cringle,
The figures move against the sky,
The clay wave breaks as they go by.
I kneeled there in the muddy fallow,
I knew that Christ was there with Callow,
That Christ was standing there with me,
That Christ had taught me what to be,
That I should plough, and as I ploughed
My Saviour Christ would sing aloud,
And as I drove the clods apart
Christ would be ploughing in my heart,
Through rest-harrow and bitter roots,
Through all my bad life's rotten fruits.

O Christ who holds the open gate,
O Christ who drives the furrow straight,
O Christ, the plough, O Christ, the laughter
Of holy white birds flying after,
Lo, all my heart's field red and torn,
And Thou wilt bring the young green corn
The young green corn divinely springing,
The young green corn for ever singing;
And when the field is fresh and fair
Thy blessèd feet shall glitter there.
And we will walk the weeded field,
And tell the golden harvest's yield,
The corn that makes the holy bread
By which the soul of man is fed,
The holy bread, the food unpriced,
Thy everlasting mercy, Christ.

John Masefield (1878–1967), from *The Everlasting Mercy*.

From friend to spouse

In this sonnet Christina Rossetti portrays Christ as a friend (John 15:13–15) who has invited us to dine, and upon whose breast, like the beloved disciple (John 13:25; 21:20), we can recline. The image is thus already of great intimacy, but Rossetti envisages yet more to come, as communion develops the relationship. For, if already a friend, what will she be in her home above?

Any notion of sin has here become subordinate, merely a passing allusion to herself as 'clod'.

> Why should I call Thee Lord, Who art my God?
>   Why should I call Thee Friend, Who art my Love?
>   Or King, Who art my very Spouse above?
> Or call Thy Sceptre on my heart Thy rod?
>   Lo, now Thy banner over me is love,
> All heaven flies open to me at Thy nod:
> For Thou hast lit Thy flame in me a clod,
>   Made me a nest for dwelling of Thy Dove.
> What wilt Thou call me in our home above,
> Who now hast called me friend? how will it be
>   When Thou for good wine settest forth the best?
> Now Thou dost bid me come and sup with Thee,
>   Now Thou dost make me lean upon Thy breast:
> How will it be with me in time of love?

Christina Rossetti (1830–94), 'After Communion'.

The first to receive

The French novelist Michel Tournier has made very effective and moving use of a Russian legend in his *The Four Wise Men* of 1982. It tells the story of an Indian prince – Taor – whose search begins flippantly, in pursuit of the perfect recipe for Turkish delight. His celebration with the older children at Bethlehem means that he misses Jesus and then the massacre of the innocents. Though he continues to keep narrowly missing an encounter with Jesus, the remainder of the story tells of Taor's spiritual transformation. Compassion for a poor debtor leads him voluntarily to undertake servitude in the salt mines of Sodom. Released at last, it is in the first eucharist that he finally encounters the Lord, after the pattern of whose life his own is now modelled.

> Where was he to go? ... First get out of the Sodom depression, climb up to the normal level of human life. Then make his way westward to Jerusalem, where he seemed most likely to find the trace of Jesus.
>
> His extreme weakness was compensated in part by his light weight. A puppet of skin and sinew, a walking skeleton, he floated over the ground as though supported by angels to the right and left of him. What gave him the greatest difficulty was the state of his eyes. A waxy pus oozed from his bleeding lids and formed thin, hard scales as it dried. Unable to face the daylight, he tore off a piece of his robe and tied it around his forehead,

leaving only a narrow rent through which he could dimly see his path.

Although the Dead Sea was well known to him, it took him seven days to reach the mouth of the Jordan. There he turned westward. On the twelfth day, he came to Bethany, the first village he had seen since his liberation. After living for thirty-three years among the Sodomites and their prisoners, he delighted in watching men, women, and children who seemed human and moved naturally in a landscape of verdure and flowers. Indeed, the sight was so refreshing that he was able to take off his blindfold. He asked one passerby and then another if he knew a prophet by the name of Jesus. The fifth person he questioned sent him to a man who was said to be a friend of Jesus. His name was Lazarus, and he lived with his sisters Martha and Mary Magdalene. Taor went to the house of this Lazarus. It was closed. A neighbour told him that this was the fourteenth day of Nisan and that many pious Jews had gone to Jerusalem to feast the Passover. Jerusalem, said the man, was less than an hour distant, and though it was already late there was a good chance of finding Jesus and his friends at the house of a certain Joseph of Arimathea.

Taor started out. At the end of the village he was overcome by weakness, for he had not eaten that day. A short while later, however, he started off again, sustained by a mysterious power.

An hour, the man had said. It took him three, and it was dark night when he entered Jerusalem. He spent quite a while looking for Joseph's house, which Lazarus' neighbour had described rather vaguely. Would he arrive too late as he had in Bethlehem, in a past which had receded to the ends of his memory? He knocked at several doors. Because it was the Feast of the Passover, the people answered gently in spite of the late hour. At last a woman opened and said yes, this was the house of Joseph of Arimathea. Yes, Jesus and his friends had met in a room on the upper storey to feast the Passover. No, she was not sure if they were still there. He could go up and see for himself.

Once again he had to climb. He had been climbing since he left the salt mine, but his legs no longer carried him. Nevertheless, he climbed and opened a door.

The room was empty. Once again he had come too late. People had eaten at this table. There were still thirteen wide, shallow goblets, each with a squat foot and two handles. In some of the goblets there were still a few drops of red wine. And on the table there were still a few pieces of the unleavened bread which the Jews eat at Passover time in memory of their fathers' flight from Egypt.

Taor's head reeled. Bread and wine! He reached for a goblet and raised it to his lips. He picked up a piece of unleavened bread and ate it. Then he toppled forward, but he did not fall. The two angels, who had been watching over him since he left the salt mines, gathered him into their great wings. The night sky opened, revealing a sea of light, and into it they bore the man who, after having been last, the eternal latecomer, had just been the first to receive the Eucharist.

Michel Tournier (b. 1924), *The Four Wise Men*,
translated by Ralph Manheim.

The snapped corn

Though not himself a Christian, Dylan Thomas was influenced by Gerard Manley Hopkins, and in content his poetry can be both pantheistic and mystical. In this particular poem he puts eucharistic imagery in reverse, as it were, to suggest humanity's destructive misappropriation of nature. The 'oat' that 'was merry' and 'the grape's joy' are made to yield to a 'flesh' that 'breaks' and 'blood' as 'desolation in the vein'. The borrowed imagery thus highlights the sacrilegious character of the way in which we treat the world and each other. Instead of our spiritual transformation being effected through the symbolic use of corn and vine, putting such things to human use can destroy both our world and us.

> This bread I break was once the oat,
> This wine upon a foreign tree
> Plunged in its fruit;
> Man in the day or wine at night
> Laid the crops low, broke the grape's joy.
>
> Once in this wine the summer blood
> Knocked in the flesh that decked the vine,
> Once in this bread
> The oat was merry in the wind;
> Man broke the sun, pulled the wind down.
>
> This flesh you break, this blood you let
> Make desolation in the vein,
> Were oat and grape

Born of the sensual root and sap;
My wine you drink, my bread you snap.

Dylan Thomas (1914–53), 'This Bread I Break'.

The empty spirit

Like Dylan Thomas, Wallace Stevens uses eucharistic imagery to pose questions to a secular society, the tone of which he sees as set by cynicism and the pursuit of money. Stevens supposes for a moment that we can associate with President Andrew Jackson, a figure of disinterested idealism who also confronted these problems, and whose statue in Washington is one of America's central monuments to its own history. But the poem's brief moment of confidence collapses into doubts and questions. To experience the sublime we need to achieve an innocence which allows us to see the world afresh. How can we do it?

How does one stand
To behold the sublime,
To confront the mockers,
The mickey mockers
And plated pairs?

When General Jackson
Posed for his statue
He knew how one feels.
Shall a man go barefoot
Blinking and blank?

But how does one feel?
One grows used to the weather,
The landscape and that;
And the sublime comes down
To the spirit itself,

The spirit and space,
The empty spirit
In vacant space.
What wine does one drink?
What bread does one eat?

Wallace Stevens (1879–1955), 'The American Sublime' from *Ideas of Order* (1936).

Soul food

Though Edward Taylor was born at Sketchly in Leicestershire, a desire to
pursue freely his Puritan commitments led him to emigrate to America,
where he was to spend most of his life as a minister to the frontier town of
Westfield, Massachusetts. His poetry was only rediscovered in the 1930s in
Yale University Library. In this poem we find in equal measure the theme of
release from sin and the soul's transformation, but these are combined with
a recurrent third emphasis, a particular understanding of the nature of
Christ's presence. A meditation on Christ's words, 'I am the living bread'
(John 6:51), the poem opens with the thought that bread is what links earth
with heaven ('the world's bright battlement'). Comparing his soul placed in
a body to a bird in a wicker cage, Taylor surmises that physical bread is of no
use to his immaterial soul, and it was only thanks to God's compassion (his
'tender bowels') that appropriate food has been given, in the form of Christ
as 'this bread of heaven', 'heaven's sugar cake'. Though the imagery is
superficially similar to that found in Andrewes and Masefield, Taylor's
analogy is carefully constructed to exclude even a hint that the materiality of
bread is relevant: it is spiritual bread feeding a spiritual soul. The intention
is, therefore, to exclude the very notion of sacramentality, but for many
readers the traditional associations of Taylor's imagery may overwhelm that
intention.

> I, kenning through astronomy divine
>> The world's bright battlement, wherein I spy
> A golden path my pencil cannot line,
>> From that bright throne unto my threshold lie.
>> And while my puzzled thoughts about it pour
>> I find the bread of life in't at my door.
>
> When that this bird of paradise put in
>> This wicker cage (my corpse) to tweedle praise
> Had pecked the fruit forbade, and so did fling
>> Away its food, and lost its golden days,
>> It fell into celestial famine sore,
>> And never could attain a morsel more.
>
> Alas! alas! poor bird, what wilt thou do?
>> The creatures' field no food for souls e'er gave;
> And if thou knock at angels' doors they show
>> An empty barrel: they no soul bread have.
>> Alas! poor bird, the world's white loaf is done,
>> And cannot yield thee here the smallest crumb.
>
> In this sad state, God's tender bowels run
>> Out streams of grace: and He, to end all strife,

The purest wheat in heaven, His dear-dear son,
    Grinds, and kneads up into this bread of life;
    Which bread of life from heaven down came and stands
    Dished on thy table up by angels' hands.

Did God mould up this bread in heaven, and bake,
    Which from His table came, and to thine goeth?
Doth He bespeak thee thus, this soul bread take.
    Come eat thy fill of this thy God's white loaf?
    It's food too fine for angels, yet come, take
    And eat thy fill. It's heaven's sugar cake.

What grace is this knead in this loaf? This thing
    Souls are but petty things it to admire.
Ye angels, help. This fill would to the brim
    Heav'ns whelmed-down crystal meal bowl, yea and
        higher.
    This bread of life dropped in thy mouth, doth cry,
    Eat, eat me, Soul, and thou shalt never die.

Edward Taylor (*c.* 1642–1729), *Meditations before the Lord's Supper*,
8 (First Series).

Hidden in the bread

On this question of how the presence of Christ in the eucharist should be understood, at the other extreme from Taylor lies the doctrine of transubstantiation, made a dogma of the Catholic Church at the Fourth Lateran Council in 1215. The concern was to insist upon the continued availability of Christ's humanity for our salvation. As one late medieval lyric puts it: 'It seems white and is red; / It is quick and seems dead; / It is flesh and seems bread; / It is one and seems two; / It is God's body and no more' ('The Sacrament of the Altar', *c.* 1450). This was sometimes interpreted in crudely literal terms, as in the story of the miracle of Bolsena at which the consecrated bread is alleged to have bled in order to convince a doubting priest, but St Thomas Aquinas offers a carefully nuanced account, and it was he who was commissioned by Pope Urban IV in 1264 to write the office of the day for the newly instituted eucharistic Feast of Corpus Christi – set to fall each year on the first Thursday after Trinity Sunday. Two of his hymns are still widely sung, 'Of the glorious body telling' and 'Thee we adore, O hidden Saviour, thee'. The latter was rendered into English verse by many poets, including Hopkins, and Richard Crashaw, whose version is given below. Associated with the Little Gidding community in the 1630s, and later a convert to Rome, from early in the Civil War Crashaw lived abroad, first in France and finally in Italy.

St Thomas's poem celebrates the mystery of the hidden God, a divinity
even in the incarnation hidden behind the humanity of Christ. The poem
ends by celebrating the life-giving sacrament using the legend of the pelican
– a traditional symbol of Christ because (according to the legend) it feeds its
young by pecking at its own breast.

> With all the powers my poor heart hath
> Of humble love and loyal faith,
> This love (my hidden life) I bow to thee,
> Whom too much love hath bowed more low for me.
> Down, down, proud sense! Discourses die!
> Keep close, my soul's enquiring eye!
> Nor touch nor taste must look for more,
> But each sit still in his own door.
>
> Your ports are all superfluous here,
> Save that which lets in faith, the ear.
> Faith is my skill. Faith can believe
> As fast as love new laws can give.
> Faith is my force. Faith strength affords
> To keep pace with those powerful words;
> And words more sure, more sweet, than they
> Love could not think, truth could not say.
>
> Oh let thy wretch find that relief
> Thou didst afford the faithful thief.
> Plead for me, love. Allege and show
> That faith has farther here to go,
> And less to lean on, because then,
> Though hid as *God*, wounds writ thee man. . . .
>
> Sweet, consider then, that I,
> Though allowed nor hand nor eye
> To reach at thy loved face, nor can
> Taste thee God or touch thee Man,
> Both yet believe; and witness thee
> My Lord too, and my God, as loud as he.
>
> Help, Lord, my faith; my hope increase;
> And fill my portion in thy peace.
> Give love for life; nor let my days
> Grow, but in new powers to thy name and praise.
>
> Oh dear memorial of that death
> Which lives still, and allows us breath!
> Rich, royal food! Bountiful bread!
> Whose use denies us to the dead;

Whose vital gust alone can give   *taste*
The same leave both to eat and live;
Live ever, bread of loves, and be
My life, my soul, my surer self to me.

O soft self-wounding Pelican,
Whose breast weeps balm for wounded man,
Ah, this way bend thy benign flood,
To a bleeding heart that gasps for blood,
That blood, whose least drops sovereign be
To wash my worlds of sin from me.
Come love! Come Lord! and that long day
For which I languish, come away,
When this dry soul those eyes shall see,
And drink the unsealed source of thee;
When glory's sun faith's shades shall chase,
And for thy veil give me thy face,
        Amen.

Richard Crashaw (1612/13–49), 'The Hymn of Saint Thomas
in Adoration of the Blessed Sacrament'.

Himself did hold

For much of Christian history (as in Orthodoxy to this day) the taking of communion was infrequent. In the Middle Ages most of the population would have done so once a year, at Easter, while in the post-Reformation Protestant churches this increased only to three or four times. In the Protestant tradition such infrequency of communion contributed to a strong emphasis upon its role as release from sin: it was an act which required careful preparation. In the Catholic tradition the mass was frequently celebrated, but the people did not often receive communion. This had consequences which may be observed in the alternative forms of piety which developed, in particular adoration of the consecrated elements of bread and wine in many ways replacing the experience of the symbolic sharing in Christ's body and blood. With this tended to go an increased stress on the paradox of worshipping what seemed so obviously inanimate.

Robert Southwell was a Jesuit missionary to England during Elizabeth I's reign, who was imprisoned and executed. He was eventually canonized in 1970. The following poem works the potential paradoxes of the eucharist to their utmost, with Christ already feeding the disciples with his own body and blood at the Last Supper and now on the altar, 'the God of hosts in slender host'. (Southwell plays on two unrelated words, the angelic hosts or army and the *hostia* or victim now lying on the sacrificial altar.)

In paschal feast the end of ancient rite
An entrance was to never-ending grace,
Types to the truth, dim glimpses to the light,
Performing deed presaging signs did chase.
Christ's final meal was fountain of our good:
For mortal meat he gave immortal food.

That which he gave he was: oh peerless gift!
Both God and man he was, and both he gave.
He in his hands himself did truly lift:
Far off they see whom in themselves they have.
Twelve did he feed; twelve did their feeder eat.
He made, he dressed, he gave, he was their meat. . . .

The God of Hosts in slender host doth dwell,
Yea, God and man, with all to either due;
The God that rules the heavens and rifled hell,
That man whose death did us to life renew;
That God and man who is the angels' bliss,
In form of bread and wine our nurture is.

Robert Southwell (1561–95), from 'Of the Blessed Sacrament of the
Altar'.

Buried in my body

In the Orthodox rite elaborate parallels between the various stages and
actions of the liturgy and the death and resurrection of Christ are drawn, as
a way of enhancing a sense of his material presence. In the Western Church
these are far less frequent, but in the late Middle Ages there began the
practice of covering the chalice and paten with a burse and veil and taking
this to symbolize the burying of Christ till the consecration brings him to
life. The practice was to become the norm in the seventeenth century. Here
the Roman Catholic poet Henry Constable takes the white host itself to be
a shroud ('sindon') for Christ's body, but once the body is placed in him, as
in a sepulchral vault ('whose monument I am') – like Christ's original
sacrifice, which freed the souls of the righteous from limbo – it can begin to
effect the soul's transformation.

When Thee (O holy sacrificèd Lamb)
In severed signs I white and liquid see,
As in thy body slain I think on Thee,
Which pale by shedding of Thy blood became;
And when again I do behold the same
Veilèd in white to be received of me,
Thou seemest in thy sindon wrapt to be
Like to a corpse, whose monument I am.

Buried in me, unto my soul appear,
Prisoned in earth, and banished from Thy sight,
Like our forefathers who in Limbo were,
Clear thou my thoughts, as thou didst give them light;
And as thou others freed from purging fire
Quench in my heart the flames of bad desire.

Henry Constable (1562–1613), 'To The Blessed Sacrament'.

The invisible meal

Jonathan Swift was an Anglican cleric and Dean of St Patrick's Cathedral in Dublin from 1713. *A Tale of a Tub* is in part the story of three brothers, Peter (representing the Church of Rome), Harry (the Anglican Church, represented by Henry VIII), and Martin (extreme Protestantism, drawing on Martin Luther). In the following extract, which reflects the norms of a fiercely contentious and not at all ecumenical age, Swift parodies the doctrine of transubstantiation. The general bitterness of Swift's satire has often led to him being described as misanthropic, but it is also possible to understand Swift's satiric violence as provoked by a strong sense of truth and justice. Certainly he was held in high regard by the ordinary people of Ireland, upon whom he regularly spent a third of his income in charitable giving.

Dining one day at an alderman's in the city, Peter observed him expatiating after the manner of his brethren, in the praises of his sirloin of beef. Beef, said the sage magistrate, is the king of meat; beef comprehends in it the quintessence of partridge, and quail, and venison, and pheasant, and plum-pudding, and custard. When Peter came home, he would needs take the fancy of cooking up this doctrine into use, and apply the precept in default of a sirloin, to his brown loaf: 'Bread,' says he, 'dear brothers, is the staff of life; in which bread is contained, inclusive, the quintessence of beef, mutton, veal, venison, partridge, plum-pudding, and custard: and to render all complete, there is intermingled a due quantity of water, whose crudities are also corrected by yeast or barm, through which means it becomes a wholesome fermented liquor diffused through the mass of the bread.' Upon the strength of these conclusions, next day at dinner was the brown loaf served up in all the formality of a city feast. 'Come brothers,' said Peter, 'fall to, and spare not; here is excellent good mutton; or hold, now my hand is in, I'll help you.' At which word, in much ceremony, with fork and knife, he carves out two good slices of a loaf, and presents each on a plate to his brothers. The elder of the two not suddenly entering into Lord Peter's conceit, began with very civil language to examine the mystery. 'My lord,' said he, 'I doubt, with great submission, there may be some mistake.' 'What,' says Peter, 'you are pleasant; come then, let us hear this jest your head is so big with.' 'None in the world, my lord; but unless I am very much deceived, your lordship was pleased a while ago to let fall a word about mutton, and I would be glad to see it with all my heart.' 'How,' said Peter, appearing in great surprise, 'I do not comprehend this at all.' – Upon which, the younger interposing to set the business right, 'My lord,' said he, 'my brother, I suppose, is hungry, and longs for the mutton your lordship hath promised us to dinner.' 'Pray,' said Peter, 'take me along with you; either you are both mad, or disposed to be merrier than I approve of; if you there do not like your piece, I will carve you another, though I should take that to be the choice bit of the whole shoulder.' 'What then, my lord,' replied the first, 'it seems this is a shoulder of mutton all this while.' 'Pray, sir,' says Peter, 'eat your victuals and leave off your impertinence, if you please, for I am not disposed to relish it at present.' But the other could not forbear, being over-provoked at the affected seriousness of Peter's countenance. 'By G—, my lord,' said he, 'I can only say, that to my eyes, and fingers, and teeth, and nose, it seems to be nothing but a crust of bread.' Upon which the second put in his word: 'I never saw a piece of mutton in my life so nearly resembling a slice from a twelve-penny loaf.' 'Look ye, gentlemen,' cries Peter in a rage, 'to convince you what a couple of blind, positive, ignorant, wilful puppies you are, I will use but this plain argument; by G—, it is true, good, natural mutton as any in Leadenhall market; and G— confound you both eternally, if you offer to believe otherwise.' Such a thundering proof as this left no farther room for objection: the two unbelievers began to gather and pocket up their mistake as hastily as they could.

Jonathan Swift (1667–1745), *A Tale of a Tub*, Section IV.

Splitting hairs

Thomas Cranmer, Archbishop of Canterbury, and principal architect of the Book of Common Prayer, was burnt at the stake in Oxford in 1556 under the Roman Catholic Queen Mary. It is, therefore, ironic that, partly because of his liturgical conservatism, and partly because of changes made in 1662, Cranmer's Prayer Book as we now know it is more Catholic than he would have liked.

Anne Ridler, herself an Anglican, takes a scholarly comment about the reasons for his death as her starting point, and questions whether Cranmer was right in his interpretation of the eucharist to be so insistent on emphasizing the commemoration of a past event – Christ's death – rather than his living or real presence under the sacramental forms of body and blood. In a manner reminiscent of Queen Elizabeth I, she suggests that, though we know not how, God must be able to enter into the matter he made.

'The bread had nothing to do with the Body – that was
what he was dying for' – Dom Gregory Dix on Cranmer

Dear Master, was it really for this you died?
      To make that separation clear,
      That heaven is elsewhere, nowise here?
That the divine, bitter yeast is not inside
      Our common bread; this body loved so
In its young crocus light, and the full orb of manhood,
      And the paean of sound, all that our senses know
Is not the matter of God?

The 'last enchantments of the Middle Age'
      In this case were a faggot fire
      And rubbish pitched beside the pyre;
A couple of burnt doors, from this so intellectual rage
      Remain, and the proposition (if dying made it plain)
Flesh turns to ashes, bread cannot turn to God.
      Yet how, if the question that caused so much pain,
Itself was wrongly made!

A change takes place: to this all can assent;
      But question 'what place does it take?
      Or none at all?' – there's the mistake,
There we confuse our terms. For this is an event
      Not subject to a physical experiment,
As water is split for energy; no gain
      In splitting hairs. We know that God can enter
To what He first contained;

We know the kingdom of heaven suffers violence,
      But not atomic. Who can weigh
      Love in a man's heart? So we still say
'Body and soul' as though they were at variance.
      Who can weigh Love? Yet sensibly he burns,

His conflagration is eyes, hands, hearts:
  So is he sensed, but in and out of the eternal,
Because the sense departs.

Anne Ridler (b. 1912), 'Cranmer and the Bread of Heaven'
from A Matter of Life and Death (1959).

The heart's tough shell

In the previous section Antonia White described how, despite Nanda's
enthusiasm and best intentions, at confirmation she still remained an 'unlit
coal'. The poet Geoffrey Hill reflects upon just such a dead experience of
the eucharist from the point of view of a communicant who is unable to
participate. The poem opens with a full acknowledgement of the power of
God: the draughts and candle flames at the service are compared with the
wind and fire that came down upon the disciples at Pentecost (Acts 2:1–4).
But the speaker, who accepts the validity of the rite, and can recall his belief
in the divine as able to confront evil, is now, like Jonah in his anger, detached
from God with no living awareness of his power. Emotionally he remains
outside the service, and eventually finds in it only coldness and a surreal
horror.

> The starched unbending candles stir
> As though a wind had caught their hair,
> As though the surging of a host
> Had charged the air of Pentecost.
> And I believe in the spurred flame,
> Those racing tongues, but cannot come
> Out of my heart's unbroken room;
> Nor feel the lips of fire among
> The cold light and the chilling song,
> The broken mouths that spill their hoard
> Of prayer like beads on to a board.
> There, at the rail, each muffled head
> Swings sombrely. O quiet deed.
> This is the breaking of the bread;
> On this the leanest heart may feed
> When by the stiffly-linened priest
> All wounds of light are newly dressed,
> Healed by the pouring-in of wine
> From bitter as from sweet grapes bled.
> But one man lay beneath his vine
> And, waking, found that it was dead.
> And so my heart has ceased to breathe
> (Though there God's worm blunted its head

And stayed.) And still I seem to smile.
Wounds have thick lips and cannot tell
If there is blackness couched beneath.
'Yet there are wounds, unquenched with oil,
And blazing eyes that would compel
Evil to turn, though like a mole
It dug blind alleys down the soil.'
So I heard once. But now I hear,
Like shifted blows at my numb back,
A grinding heel; a scraped chair.
The heart's tough shell is still to crack
When, spent of all its wine and bread,
Unwinkingly the altar lies
Wreathed in its sour breath, cold and dead.
A server has put out its eyes.

Geoffrey Hill (b. 1932), 'The Bidden Guest' from *For the
Unfallen* (1959).

Too cruel a demand

In 1878 Leo Tolstoy experienced an emotional and intellectual crisis that
was to lead to his conversion to Christianity. Four years later he produced an
account of this in *A Confession*, though the censor forbade its publication at
the time, a fate shared by many of the other radical writings which were to
stem from this change of perspective. The following extract shows Tolstoy
intensely engaged by his own understanding of the communion service – a
legitimate understanding, though he is in retrospect prepared to criticize it.
But he is repelled by the Orthodox Church's insistence on the real presence
of Christ's humanity in the eucharist, which he cannot accept. His solution
to this dilemma is a sharp rejection of intellectual questions in favour of a
faith which is more experiential and imaginative.

> It was then so necessary for me to believe in order to live that I
> unconsciously concealed from myself the contradictions and
> obscurities of theology. But this reading of meanings into the
> rites had its limits. ... Quite two-thirds of all the services –
> either remained completely incomprehensible or, when I forced
> an explanation into them, made me feel that I was lying, thereby
> quite destroying my relation to God and depriving me of all
> possibility of belief.
>
> I felt the same about the celebration of the chief holi-
> days. ...
>
> At the celebration of these holidays, feeling that importance
> was being attributed to the very things that to me presented a

negative importance, I either devised tranquillizing explana-
tions or shut my eyes in order not to see what tempted me.

Most of all this happened to me when taking part in the most
usual Sacraments, which are considered the most important:
baptism and communion. There I encountered not incompre-
hensible but fully comprehensible doings: doings which seemed
to me to lead into temptation, and I was in a dilemma – whether
to lie or to reject them.

Never shall I forget the painful feeling I experienced the day I
received the Eucharist for the first time after many years. The
service, confession, and prayers were quite intelligible and
produced in me a glad consciousness that the meaning of life
was being revealed to me. The Communion itself I explained as
an act performed in remembrance of Christ, and indicating a
purification from sin and the full acceptance of Christ's teaching. If that explanation was artificial I did not notice its
artificiality: so happy was I at humbling and abasing myself
before the priest – a simple, timid country clergyman – turning
all the dirt out of my soul and confessing my vices, so glad was I
to merge in thought with the humility of the fathers who wrote
the prayers of the office, so glad was I of union with all who have
believed and now believe, that I did not notice the artificiality of
my explanation. But when I approached the altar gates, and the
priest made me say that I believed that what I was about to
swallow was truly flesh and blood, I felt a pain in my heart: it was
not merely a false note, it was a cruel demand made by someone
or other who evidently had never known what faith is.

I now permit myself to say that it was a cruel demand, but I did
not then think so: only it was indescribably painful to me. I was
no longer in the position in which I had been in youth when I
thought all in life was clear; I had indeed come to faith because,
apart from faith, I had found nothing, certainly nothing, except
destruction; therefore to throw away that faith was impossible
and I submitted. And I found in my soul a feeling which helped
me to endure it. This was the feeling of self-abasement and
humility. I humbled myself, swallowed that flesh and blood
without any blasphemous feelings and with a wish to believe.
But the blow had been struck and, knowing what awaited me, I
could not go a second time.

I continued to fulfil the rites of the Church and still believed
that the doctrine I was following contained the truth, when
something happened to me which I now understand but which

then seemed strange.

I was listening to the conversation of an illiterate peasant, a pilgrim, about God, faith, life, and salvation, when a knowledge of faith revealed itself to me. I drew near to the people, listening to their opinions on life and faith, and I understood the truth more and more. So also was it when I read the Lives of Holy Men, which became my favourite books. Putting aside the miracles and regarding them as fables illustrating thoughts, this reading revealed to me life's meaning. There were the lives of Makarius the Great, the story of Buddha, there were the words of St John Chrysostom, and there were the stories of the traveller in the well, the monk who found some gold, and of Peter the publican. There were stories of the martyrs, all announcing that death does not exclude life, and there were the stories of ignorant, stupid men, who knew nothing of the teaching of the Church but who yet were saved.

But as soon as I met learned believers or took up their books, doubt of myself, dissatisfaction, and exasperated disputation were roused within me, and I felt that the more I entered into the meaning of these men's speech, the more I went astray from truth and approached an abyss.

Leo Tolstoy (1828–1910), A Confession, chapter 14,
translated by Aylmer Maude.

In flows heaven

Difficulties of belief are, of course, often either intensified or alleviated by the context in which the rite is celebrated. This fact provides one common justification for ritual, that it can augment the sense of Christ's presence; the sacramentality of the bread and wine is reinforced by all one's senses together speaking of that divine mystery.

The Anglican Robert Browning captures something of this in his description of a eucharistic celebration in Rome. The winding columns of the canopy over the altar (the 'baldachin'), the candles ('the taper fires') and the incense are all reminders of heaven as they point upwards, until the bell that announces the consecration pulls one down once more, when 'in flows heaven' and with it 'very man and very God'. However, this is only one of three versions of Christmas Eve which the poem presents; it is set between a poor and Protestant one in an English chapel of 'gospel simplicity' and an intellectual and rationalist one in a German university; and it is the English one which is finally preferred.

I, the sinner that speak to you,
Was in Rome this night, and stood, and knew
Both this and more. For see, for see,
The dark is rent, mine eye is free
To pierce the crust of the outer wall,
And I view inside, and all there, all,
As the swarming hollow of a hive,
The whole Basilica alive!
Men in the chancel, body and nave,
Men on the pillars' architrave,
Men on the statues, men on the tombs
With popes and kings in their porphyry wombs,
All famishing in expectation
Of the main-altar's consummation.
For see, for see, the rapturous moment
Approaches, and earth's best endowment
Blends with heaven's; the taper-fires
Pant up, the winding brazen spires
Heave loftier yet the baldachin;
The incense-gaspings, long kept in,
Suspire in clouds; the organ blatant
Holds his breath and grovels latent,
As if God's hushing finger grazed him,
(Like Behemoth when he praised him)
At the silver bell's shrill tinkling,
Quick cold drops of terror sprinkling
On the sudden pavement strewed
With faces of the multitude.
Earth breaks up, time drops away,
In flows heaven, with its new day
Of endless life, when He who trod,
Very man and very God,
This earth in weakness, shame and pain,
Dying the death whose signs remain
Up yonder on the accursed tree, –
Shall come again, no more to be
Of captivity the thrall,
But the one God, All in all,
King of kings, Lord of lords,
As His servant John received the words,
'I died, and live for evermore!'

        Robert Browning (1812–89), from *Christmas-Eve*.

No religion of forms

Whatever his final conclusion, Browning's poetry leaves no doubt about the sympathy he felt for ritual. The same cannot be said for the American philosopher and poet Ralph Waldo Emerson. After several years as a Unitarian minister he resigned because of doubts over the celebration of the Lord's Supper. He questioned whether Christ had intended it to be a permanent institution, and also whether it did not detract from the worship of God by giving too strong a focus upon Christ. But, as this extract reveals, the heart of his objection strikes at a sacramental understanding of the world. Taking his cue from Romans 14:17, he argues that the essence of Christianity is its morality, and not forms or symbols, which belong to more primitive versions of religion.

> Passing other objections, I come to this, that the *use of the elements*, however suitable to the people and the modes of thought in the East, where it originated, is foreign and unsuited to affect us. Whatever long usage and strong association may have done in some individuals to deaden this repulsion, I apprehend that their use is rather tolerated than loved by any of us. We are not accustomed to express our thoughts or emotions by symbolical actions. Most men find the bread and wine no aid to devotion and to some, it is a painful impediment. To eat bread is one thing; to love the precepts of Christ and resolve to obey them is quite another. . . .
>
> I am not so foolish as to declaim against forms. Forms are as essential as bodies; but to exalt particular forms, to adhere to one form a moment after it is out-grown, is unreasonable, and it is alien to the spirit of Christ. If I understand the distinction of Christianity, the reason why it is to be preferred over all other systems and is divine is this, that it is a moral system; that it presents men with truths which are their own reason, and enjoins practices that are their own justification; that if miracles may be said to have been its evidence to the first Christians, they are not its evidence to us, but the doctrines themselves; that every practice is Christian which praises itself, and every practice unchristian which condemns itself. I am not engaged to Christianity by decent forms, or saving ordinances; it is not usage, it is not what I do not understand, that binds me to it – let these be the sandy foundations of falsehoods. What I revere and obey in it is its reality, its boundless charity, its deep interior life, the rest it gives to my mind, the echo it returns to my thoughts, the perfect accord it makes with my reason through all its representation of God and His Providence; and the persuasion

and courage that come out thence to lead me upward and onward. Freedom is the essence of this faith. It has for its object simply to make men good and wise. Its institutions, then, should be as flexible as the wants of men. That form out of which the life and suitableness have departed, should be as worthless in its eyes as the dead leaves that are falling around us. . . .

The Jewish was a religion of forms. The Pagan was a religion of forms; it was all body – it had no life – and the Almighty God was pleased to qualify and send forth a man to teach men that they must serve him with the heart; that only that life was religious which was thoroughly good; that sacrifice was smoke, and forms were shadows.

Ralph Waldo Emerson (1803–82), from his sermon 'The Lord's Supper'.

After-shave and High Mass

In this short extract from his blank verse autobiography of his early life, *Summoned by Bells*, John Betjeman initially traps the reader by reminding us of the joy we often experience in celebrating our own physicality, whether it be with after-shave or a fine cut of marmalade. For him Anglo-Catholic religious ritual is an extension of this, a celebration of God entering into that physicality. This is something which was true for him from his earliest years at the Dragon School, Oxford, to his time as a university student there, attending one of its chapels founded in honour of E. B. Pusey, one of the leaders of the Oxford Movement.

> Silk-dressing-gowned, to Sunday-morning bells,
> Long after breakfast had been cleared in Hall,
> I wandered to my lavender-scented bath;
> Then, with a loosely knotted shantung tie
> And hair well soaked in Delhez' Genêt d'Or,
> Strolled to the Eastgate. Oxford marmalade
> And a thin volume by Lowes Dickinson
> But half-engaged my thoughts till Sunday calm
> Led me by crumbling walls and echoing lanes,
> Past college chapels with their organ-groan
> And churches stacked with bicycles outside,
> To worship at High Mass in Pusey House.
>
> Those were the days when that divine baroque
> Transformed our English altars and our ways.
> Fiddle-back chasuble in mid-Lent pink
> Scandalized Rome and Protestants alike:
> 'Why do you try to ape the Holy See?'
> 'Why do you sojourn in a halfway house?'

And if these doubts had ever troubled me
(Praise God, they don't) I would have made the move.
What seemed to me a greater question then
Tugged and still tugs: Is Christ the Son of God?
Despite my frequent lapses into lust,
Despite hypocrisy, revenge and hate,
I learned at Pusey House the Catholic faith.
Friends of those days, now patient parish priests,
By worldly standards you have not 'got on'
Who knelt with me as Oxford sunlight streamed
On some colonial bishop's broidered cope.
Some know for all their lives that Christ is God,
Some start upon that arduous love affair
In clouds of doubt and argument; and some
(My closest friends) seem not to want His love –
And why this is I wish to God I knew.
As at the Dragon School, so still for me
The steps to truth were made by sculptured stone,
Stained glass and vestments, holy-water stoups,
Incense and crossings of myself – the things
That hearty middle-stumpers most despise
As 'all the inessentials of the Faith'.

John Betjeman (1906–84), from Summoned by Bells.

The ritual of shop and street

In this sonnet the American poet, social commentator and Baptist minister
Robert Whitaker does not deny the importance of ritual but urges us to
perceive the sacramental in all of life and not just in the narrow, church
context – in the natural world, and even (he comments paradoxically) in
passages of scripture to which we have become dulled by rote learning.
Then an ordinary meal will convey a sense of the presence of God no less
than the formal ritual of communion.

Teach me the ritual that runs beyond
   The rote of words, the flexing of the knee:
   Let me be always, Lord of Life, with Thee!
In all my motions ready to respond
To Thy unveilings, though in Scripture conned,
   Or in the mid-night's insect melody,
   The scent of bloom from desert bush or tree,
The dawn's reflection in the blushing pond.
How shall I worship only for an hour?
How think Thee present under dome and spire

Or sense Thee in the wafer and the wine
Except the common bread and cup are Thine,
Thine shop and street, the hearth-stone and the fire,
Thine all the ministries of natural power?

                                    Robert Whitaker (1863–1944).

Quickening dry stubble

Henry Vaughan, like his twin brother Thomas, was a mystic, attracted by the idea of sympathetic bonds uniting microcosm and macrocosm. Such an idea lends itself to a sacramental understanding of the world. Holy Communion is therefore seen by Vaughan as the natural culmination of God's work through the created order. Here then is an answer to Emerson, and others who protest the irrelevance of symbols to Christianity. Yet for Vaughan often these material symbols and rituals work paradoxically. Thus, just as the darkness at Christ's death (Mark 15:33) brought us greater light, so now in the eucharist the shepherd feeds us on himself with body and blood that have become as delightful as the flowers that adorn the valley (Song of Songs 2:1).

Welcome sweet, and sacred feast; welcome life!
    Dead I was, and deep in trouble;
But grace and blessings came with thee so rife,
    That they have quickenèd even dry stubble;
        Thus souls their bodies animate,
        And thus, at first, when things were rude,
            Dark, void, and crude,
        They, by thy Word, their beauty had and date;
            All were by thee,
            And still must be,
        Nothing that is, or lives,
But hath his quickenings and reprieves,
        As thy hand opes, or shuts;
            Healings and cuts,
Darkness and day-light, life and death,
Are but mere leaves turned by thy breath.
        Spirits without thee die,
            And blackness sits
        On the divinest wits,
As on the sun eclipses lie.
But that great darkness at thy death,
When the veil broke with thy last breath,
            Did make us see
            The way to thee;

And now by these sure, sacred ties,
    After thy blood
    (Our sovereign good)
    Had cleared our eyes,
    And given us sight,
Thou dost unto thyself betroth
  Our souls and bodies both,
  In everlasting light.

Was't not enough that thou hadst paid the price,
    And given us eyes
When we had none, but thou must also take
    Us by the hand,
    And keep us still awake
    When we would sleep,
    Or from thee creep,
Who without thee cannot stand?
Was't not enough to lose thy breath
And blood by an accursèd death,
  But thou must also leave,
  To us, that did bereave
Thee of them both, these seals, the means
  That should both cleanse
    And keep us so,
    Who wrought thy woe?
O rose of *Sharon*! O the lily
    Of the valley!
How art thou now, thy flock to keep,
Become both *food*, and *shepherd* to thy sheep.

Henry Vaughan (1621–95), 'The Holy Communion'.

MINISTERS OF GRACE

Introduction

Though Jesus' commissioning of the twelve disciples lacks such detail (Mark 3:13ff.), in ordaining some individuals to certain specific tasks through the laying on of hands the early Church could point to clear Old Testament precedents (e.g. Num 27:18), and this seems quickly to have become the norm (e.g. Acts 6:6). Some passages seem to imply the conveying of special grace: 'the gift of God that is within you through the laying on of my hands' (2 Tim 1:6). The more this is stressed, the more Christian ministry will be seen as having a sacramental character, with the ordained person viewed as a medium through which God chooses to act. The Eastern Orthodox have always insisted that the Church as a whole shares in this ministry, with even baptism seen as a form of ordination (hands are laid on the child and it is vested in a white robe, paralleling priestly vestments). But in the Western tradition a gradual concentration or narrowing of focus took place.

In the early Middle Ages ordinations to offices such as reader or door keeper were still seen as sacramental acts, but gradually an almost exclusive stress came to be placed upon the right to offer the sacrifice of the mass – symbolized in the giving of a chalice and paten to the newly ordained priest. That focus is reflected in the first extract from the late medieval play *Everyman*, whereas the next three passages widen (Dryden, following Chaucer) or correct this conception (Herbert, Longfellow). Though the minister continues to have a distinctive role, it is now as mediator of Christ's teaching, example and care. This, it should be stressed, is not to abandon a sacramental understanding. Rather, it is to identify a different way of mediating Christ's presence, through a pattern of life rather than specific sacramental acts.

The more, however, this latter conception is stressed, the easier it is for the clergy to fall short of the ideal. In part such failures can be explained by unsuitable candidates pursuing what was seen as both a lucrative and a socially acceptable occupation. The results can be observed in some of Jane Austen's clergy, as also in the Milton and Brontë extracts here. Sometimes self-deception played its part (Trollope, Butler), but undoubtedly a lack of realism about what might plausibly be expected of another human being should also be seen as an important factor. Goldsmith's *Deserted Village* allows no chink in the armour of virtue, whereas Jennings concedes that the burden may be too great for any one person, while for Browning even doubt finds its place in the clerical vocation. It is in view of the vocation's difficulties that R. S. Thomas advises we trust God to effect his purposes through his clergy in his good time, not in theirs or ours.

Above angels in degree

Everyman is the best known of all the morality plays, and is usually assigned a date in the late fifteenth or early sixteenth century. Here the priest is mediator of the traditional seven sacraments, especially of the eucharist with its 'five words' of consecration – *hoc est enim corpus meum* – and of the absolution of sin in penance – 'the priest bindeth and unbindeth all bands' (cf. Matt 16:19). But that very privilege and power – greater than that of 'any angel ... in heaven' – makes all the more despicable the priest's corruption in financial or sexual sin.

> *Five Wits*. There is no emperor, king, duke, ne baron,
> That of God hath commission
> As hath the least priest in the world being;   *living*
> For of the blessed sacraments pure and benign
> He beareth the keys, and thereof hath cure   *charge*
> For man's redemption it is ever sure,
> Which God for our soul's medicine
> Gave us out of his heart with great pain.
> Here in this transitory life, for thee and me
> The blessèd sacraments seven there be:
> Baptism, confirmation, with priesthood good,
> And the sacrament of God's precious flesh and blood,
> Marriage, the holy extreme unction, and penance;
> These seven be good to have in remembrance,
> Gracious sacraments of high divinity.
> *Everyman*. Fain would I receive that holy body,
> And meekly to my ghostly father I will go.   *spiritual*
> *Five Wits*. Everyman, that is the best that ye can do.
> God will you to salvation bring,
> For priesthood exceedeth all other thing:
> To us Holy Scripture they do teach,
> And converteth man from sin heaven to reach;
> God hath to them more power given
> Than to any angel that is in heaven.
> With five words he may consecrate,

God's body in flesh and blood to make,
And handleth his Maker between his hands.
The priest bindeth and unbindeth all bands,
Both in earth and in heaven.
Thou ministers all the sacraments seven;   *administer*
Though we kissed thy feet, thou were worthy;
Thou art the surgeon that cureth sin deadly:
No remedy we find under God
But alone in priesthood.
Everyman, God gave priests that dignity,
And setteth them in his stead among us to be;
Thus be they above angels in degree.

[*Everyman goes to the priest to receive the last sacraments*]

   Knowledge. If priests be good it is so, surely.
But when Jesus hanged on the cross with great smart,
There gave he out of his blessèd heart
The same sacrament in great torment:
He sold them not to us, that Lord omnipotent.
Therefore Saint Peter the apostle doth say
That Jesu's curse have all they
Which God their Saviour do buy or sell,
Or they for any money do take or tell.   *count out*
Sinful priests giveth the sinners example bad;
Their children sitteth by other men's fires, I have heard;
And some haunteth women's company
With unclean life, as lusts of lechery:
These be with sin made blind.
   Five Wits. I trust to God no such may we find;
Therefore let us priesthood honour,
And follow their doctrine for our souls' succour.
We be their sheep, and they shepherds be,
By whom we all be kept in surety.

                From the play *Everyman*.

Another head, another heart

A common Reformation objection to the view of the priestly function
portrayed in *Everyman* was that it could be taken to imply that ordination
bestows powers which can be exercised independently of God. Herbert was
a priest of the Church of England for only the last three years of his life,
dying of consumption shortly before his fortieth birthday. In this poem, a
meditation on the detailed instructions given in Exodus 28 for the vesting of

Aaron (Moses' brother and chief priest of the Israelites), Herbert is careful
to insist that everything he does as a priest he does only in and through
Christ acting in him. In the Exodus passage much is made of the breast-
plate, and Herbert contrasts his own troubled breast with the harmony and
music which Christ can give when he is the priest's head. Aaron had 'bells
of gold' round the hem of his robe; even when the priest feels spiritually
dead, Herbert suggests, Christ can 'tune' his bells, and so enable him
properly to fulfil the priestly function.

> Holiness on the head,
> Light and perfections on the breast,
> Harmonious bells below, raising the dead
> To lead them unto life and rest:
> Thus are true Aarons dressed.
>
> Profaneness in my head,
> Defects and darkness in my breast,
> A noise of passions ringing me for dead
> Unto a place where is no rest:
> Poor priest thus am I dressed.
>
> Only another head
> I have, another heart and breast,
> Another music, making live not dead,
> Without whom I could have no rest:
> In him I am well dressed.
>
> Christ is my only head,
> My alone only heart and breast,
> My only music, striking me ev'n dead,
> That to the old man I may rest,
> And be in him new dressed.
>
> So holy in my head,
> Perfect and light in my dear breast,
> My doctrine tuned by Christ (who is not dead,
> But lives in me while I do rest),
> Come people, Aaron's dressed.

George Herbert (1593–1633), 'Aaron' from *The Temple*.

Patterns for the rest

The Catholic tradition has generally seen the priest's primary role as
mediator of sacraments, while the Protestant has placed greater stress on
the role of the minister as teacher and example. Nonetheless, it would be
absurd to suggest that the latter conception has played no role in the

Catholic understanding of priesthood. Dryden became a Roman Catholic in 1686. Though in part he uses this translation of Chaucer as a pretext for enlarging upon his own belief in the divine right of kings (James II having been recently overthrown in the so-called 'Glorious Revolution' of 1688), he also follows closely Chaucer's intentions, and expresses an ideal of priest-hood which has remained consistent over the centuries, for Catholic as much as for Protestant. Moreover, it is no less sacramental in its conception. Through his own life being 'impressed' so that he becomes heaven's 'precious coin' (showing his sovereign's likeness), the priest can mediate the pattern intended for all Christians.

> A parish priest was of the pilgrim train:
> An awful, reverend, and religious man.
> His eyes diffused a venerable grace,
> And Charity itself was in his face.
> Rich was his soul, though his attire was poor
> (As God had clothed his own ambassador),
> For such, on earth, his blessed Redeemer bore.
> Of sixty years he seemed, and well might last
> To sixty more, but that he lived too fast;
> Refined himself to soul to curb the sense,
> And made almost a sin of abstinence.
> Yet had his aspect nothing of severe,
> But such a face as promised him sincere.
> Nothing reserved or sullen was to see,
> But sweet regards and pleasing sanctity:
> Mild was his accent, and his action free.
> With eloquence innate his tongue was armed;
> Though harsh the precept, yet the preacher charmed.
> For, letting down the golden chain from high,
> He drew his audience upward to the sky:
> And oft with holy hymns he charmed their ears,
> A music more melodious than the spheres;
> For David left him, when he went to rest,
> His lyre; and after him, he sung the best.
> He bore his great commission in his look,
> But sweetly tempered awe, and softened all he spoke.
> He preached the joys of heaven, and pains of hell,
> And warned the sinner with becoming zeal;
> But on eternal mercy loved to dwell.
> He taught the Gospel rather than the Law:
> And forced himself to drive, but loved to draw.
> For fear but freezes minds; but love, like heat,

Exhales the soul sublime to seek her native seat. . . .
True priests, he said, and preachers of the Word,
Were only stewards of their sovereign Lord;
Nothing was theirs, but all the public store,
Entrusted riches to relieve the poor;
Who, should they steal, for want of his relief,
He judged himself accomplice with the thief.
Wide was his parish, not contracted close
In streets, but here and there a straggling house;
Yet still he was at hand, without request,
To serve the sick, to succour the distressed;
Tempting, on foot, alone, without affright,
The dangers of a dark, tempestuous night.
All this the good old man performed alone,
Nor spared his pains, for curate he had none.
Nor durst he trust another with his care,
Nor rode himself to Paul's, the public fair,
To chaffer for preferment with his gold,
Where bishoprics and sinecures are sold.
But duly watched his flock by night and day,
And from the prowling wolf redeemed the prey,
And hungry sent the wily fox away.
The proud he tamed, the penitent he cheered,
Nor to rebuke the rich offender feared.
His preaching much, but more his practice wrought,
A living sermon of the truths he taught;
For this by rules severe his life he squared,
That all might see the doctrine which they heard.
For priests, he said, are patterns for the rest,
The gold of heaven, who bear the God impressed;
But when the precious coin is kept unclean,
The sovereign's image is no longer seen.
If they be foul on whom the people trust,
Well may the baser brass contract a rust.

John Dryden (1631–1700), *The Character of a Good Parson:
Imitated from Chaucer and Enlarged.*

Invisible hands at work

The Protestant Longfellow here extends to pastoral care a similar conception of Christ operating sacramentally in and through the Church's
ministers. He sees in the hands laid on his brother's head at ordination the
'invisible hands' of Christ. That unseen presence will then continue to be

active throughout his ministry, patterned on that of Christ (including the contrasting events of Cana and Gethsemane), enabling him to care more effectively for his parishioners in both their joys and their sorrows. The relationship between the ordained and Christ must be as close as that of the beloved disciple to his Lord in the fourth gospel (John 13:23).

> Christ to the young man said: 'Yet one thing more;
>   If thou wouldst perfect be,
> Sell all thou hast and give it to the poor,
>   And come and follow me!'
>
> Within this temple Christ again, unseen,
>   Those sacred words hath said,
> And his invisible hands today have been
>   Laid on a young man's head.
>
> And evermore beside him on his way
>   The unseen Christ shall move,
> That he may lean upon his arm and say,
>   'Dost thou, dear Lord, approve?'
>
> Beside him at the marriage feast shall be,
>   To make the scene more fair;
> Beside him in the dark Gethsemane
>   Of pain and midnight prayer.
>
> O holy trust! O endless sense of rest!
>   Like the beloved John
> To lay his head upon the Saviour's breast,
>   And thus to journey on!

Henry Wadsworth Longfellow (1807–82), 'Hymn for my
Brother's Ordination'.

The wolf's paw

Clergy have, of course, not always lived up to the sacramental ideals of which previous extracts have spoken. *Everyman* pointed at failures among the pre-Reformation clergy, while the Chaucer/Dryden ideal is built up by implied contrasts with actual corruptions. Milton's *Lycidas* was written in 1637, not long after Herbert's death, to commemorate a Cambridge contemporary (the 'young swain'), a candidate for ordination who had been drowned at sea. The last appearance of the Risen Christ in John's Gospel is to Simon Peter by the Sea of Galilee or Tiberias, and there Christ gives his final instruction, 'Feed my sheep' (John 21:17). Milton here uses this analogy as a pretext to complain of the lack of pastoral care and the general corruption shown by the Anglican clergy of his time.

Last came, and last did go,
The Pilot of the Galilean lake;
Two massy keys he bore of metals twain
(The golden opes, the iron shuts amain).
He shook his mitred locks, and stern bespake:
'How well could I have spared for thee, young swain,
Enow of such as for their bellies' sake
Creep and intrude and climb into the fold!
Of other care they little reck'ning make
Than how to scramble at the shearers' feast,
And shove away the worthy bidden guest.
Blind mouths! that scarce themselves know how to hold
A sheep-hook, or have learned aught else the least
That to the faithful herdman's art belongs!
What recks it them? What need they? They are sped;
And when they list, their lean and flashy songs
Grate on their scrannel pipes of wretched straw;
The hungry sheep look up, and are not fed,
But swoln with wind, and the rank mist they draw,
Rot inwardly, and foul contagion spread;
Besides what the grim wolf with privy paw
Daily devours apace, and nothing said;
But that two-handed engine at the door
Stands ready to smite once, and smite no more.'

John Milton (1608–74), from *Lycidas*.

A zeal to drink tea

Though the social status of the clergy meant that sometimes the position was often as no more than an opening for the younger sons of the gentry or aspiring middle-class, historians would now generally regard Milton's account as exaggerated. Nonetheless, it is true that the later nineteenth century saw a fresh enthusiasm for pastoral care, particularly through Pusey's leadership of the Oxford or Anglo-Catholic movement. The replacement of the black gown with a white surplice for worship was seen by Charlotte Brontë as part of this.

In this extract from her second novel, *Shirley*, published in 1849, contemporary standards are contrasted with those of the beginning of the century when, she alleges, 'youthful Levites' (an allusion to the priestly tribe in ancient Israel) were more interested in frivolities, despite the appalling conditions prevailing in the Yorkshire mills, not far from her parsonage home at Haworth.

Of late years an abundant shower of curates has fallen upon
the north of England: but in eighteen-hundred-eleven-twelve

that affluent rain had not descended: curates were scarce then: there was no Pastoral Aid – no Additional Curates' Society to stretch a helping hand to worn-out old rectors and incumbents, and give them the wherewithal to pay a vigorous young colleague from Oxford or Cambridge. The present successors of the apostles, disciples of Dr Pusey and tools of the Propaganda, were at that time being hatched under cradle-blankets, or undergoing regeneration by nursery-baptism in wash-hand-basins. You could not have guessed by looking at any one of them that the Italian-ironed double frills of its net-cap surrounded the brows of a preordained, specially sanctified successor of St Paul, St Peter, or St John; nor could you have foreseen in the folds of its long night-gown the white surplice in which it was hereafter cruelly to exercise the souls of its parishioners, and strangely to nonplus its old-fashioned vicar by flourishing aloft in a pulpit the shirt-like raiment which had never before waved higher than the reading-desk.

Yet even in those days of scarcity there were curates: the precious plant was rare, but it might be found. A certain favoured district in the West Riding of Yorkshire could boast three rods of Aaron blossoming within a circuit of twenty miles. ...

These gentlemen are in the bloom of youth; they possess all the activity of that interesting age – an activity which their moping old vicars would fain turn into the channel of their pastoral duties, often expressing a wish to see it expended in a diligent superintendence of the schools, and in frequent visits to the sick of their respective parishes. But the youthful Levites feel this to be dull work; they prefer lavishing their energies on a course of proceeding, which, though to other eyes it appear more heavy with ennui, more cursed with monotony, than the toil of the weaver at his loom, seems to yield them an unfailing supply of enjoyment and occupation.

I allude to a rushing backwards and forwards, amongst themselves, to and from their respective lodgings: not a round – but a triangle of visits, which they keep up all the year through, in winter, spring, summer, and autumn. Season and weather make no difference; with unintelligible zeal they dare snow and hail, wind and rain, mire and dust, to go and dine, or drink tea, or sup with each other. What attracts them, it would be difficult to say. It is not friendship; for whenever they meet they quarrel. It is not religion; the thing is never named amongst them: theology they may discuss occasionally, but piety – never.

Charlotte Brontë (1816–55), *Shirley*, chapter 1.

Clerical ambition

Barchester Towers was published in 1857, the second of Trollope's six clerical novels, the Barsetshire sequence. Obadiah Slope, the bishop's chaplain, and Mrs Proudie, his wife, are two powerful personalities, locked in battle, trying to secure the vacant wardenship of Hiram's Hospital for rival candidates. Slope wants it for the saintly Mr Harding because thereby he hopes to secure the hand and fortune of Harding's widowed daughter. The corruption of the clerical mind through ambition is finely (and hilariously) drawn, with the aptly named Mr Quiverful (with his fourteen children) a highly effective foil to the machinations of Slope. The fact that not just Slope but almost all evangelical clergy are pilloried by Trollope tells us more about the author than it does about the general behaviour of such clergy in Victorian England. Indeed Pastoral Aid (mentioned by Brontë) tells a very different tale, of a group concerned to fund additional clergy.

> Mr Harding had another friend fighting his battle for him, quite as powerful as the master of Lazarus, and this was Mr Slope. Though the bishop had so pertinaciously insisted on giving way to his wife in the matter of the hospital, Mr Slope did not think it necessary to abandon his object. He had, he thought, daily more and more reason to imagine that the widow would receive his overtures favourably, and he could not but feel that Mr Harding at the hospital, and placed there by his means, would be more likely to receive him as a son-in-law, than Mr Harding growling in opposition and disappointment under the archdeacon's wing at Plumstead. Moreover, to give Mr Slope due credit, he was actuated by greater motives even than these. He wanted a wife, and he wanted money, but he wanted power more than either. He had fully realized the fact that he must come to blows with Mrs Proudie. He had no desire to remain in Barchester as her chaplain. Sooner than do so, he would risk the loss of his whole connection with the diocese. What! was he to feel within him the possession of no ordinary talents; was he to know himself to be courageous, firm, and, in matters where his conscience did not interfere, unscrupulous; and yet be contented to be the working factotum of a woman-prelate? Mr Slope had higher ideas of his own destiny. Either he or Mrs Proudie must go to the wall; and now had come the time when he would try which it should be.

The bishop had declared that Mr Quiverful should be the new warden. As Mr Slope went downstairs prepared to see the archdeacon if necessary, but fully satisfied that no such necessity would arise, he declared to himself that Mr Harding should be warden. With the object of carrying his point, he rode over to Puddingdale, and had a further interview with the worthy expectant of clerical good things. . . .

Mr Slope was all smiles as he shook his brother clergyman's hand, and said that he had ridden over because he thought it right at once to put Mr Quiverful in possession of the facts of the matter regarding the wardenship of the hospital. As he spoke, the poor expectant husband and father saw at a glance that his brilliant hopes were to be dashed to the ground, and that his visitor was now there for the purpose of unsaying what on his former visit he had said. . . .

'You will remember that I told you that Mr Harding had refused to return to the hospital.'

Mr Quiverful declared that nothing could be more distinct on his memory.

'And acting on this refusal, I suggested that you should take the hospital,' continued Mr Slope.

'I understood you to say that the bishop had authorized you to offer it to me.'

'Did I? did I go so far as that? Well, perhaps it may be, that in my anxiety in your behalf I did commit myself further than I should have done. So far as my own memory serves me, I don't think I did go quite so far as that. But I own I was very anxious that you should get it; and I may have said more than was quite prudent.'

'But,' said Mr Quiverful, in his deep anxiety to prove his case, 'my wife received as distinct a promise from Mrs Proudie as one human being could give to another.'

Mr Slope smiled, and gently shook his head. He meant that smile for a pleasant smile, but it was diabolical in the eyes of the man he was speaking to. 'Mrs Proudie!' he said. 'If we are to go to what passes between the ladies in these matters, we shall really be in a nest of troubles from which we shall never extricate ourselves. Mrs Proudie is a most excellent lady, kind-hearted, charitable, pious, and in every way estimable. But, my dear Mr Quiverful, the patronage of the diocese is not in her hands.'

Anthony Trollope (1815–82), Barchester Towers, chapter 24.

A guided vocation

Published posthumously in 1903, *The Way of All Flesh* reflects some aspects of Butler's own life. Grandson of a bishop and son of a priest, like the hero of his novel he too had been pressed to follow in his father's footsteps. But there the resemblance ends, since Butler himself escaped ordination. In this extract the point of the satire is clear, unlike some of his earlier efforts where it was so gentle that some contemporary readers missed the joke entirely. But that perhaps was the point, since Butler's primary aim was to parody self-deception about one's real motives.

> 'MY DEAR FATHER. – I do not like opening up a question which has been considered settled, but as the time approaches I begin to be very doubtful how far I am fitted to be a clergyman. Not, I am thankful to say, that I have the faintest doubts about the Church of England, and I could subscribe cordially to every one of the thirty-nine articles which do indeed appear to me to be the *ne plus ultra* of human wisdom, and Paley, too, leaves no loop-hole for an opponent; but I am sure I should be running counter to your wishes if I were to conceal from you that I do not feel the inward call to be a minister of the gospel that I shall have to say I have felt when the Bishop ordains me. I try to get this feeling, I pray for it earnestly, and sometimes half think that I have got it, but in a little time it wears off, and though I have no absolute repugnance to being a clergyman and trust that if I am one I shall endeavour to live to the Glory of God and to advance His interests upon earth, yet I feel that something more than this is wanted before I am fully justified in going into the Church. I am aware that I have been a great expense to you in spite of my scholarships, but you have ever taught me that I should obey my conscience, and my conscience tells me I should do wrong if I became a clergyman. God may yet give me the spirit for which I assure you I have been and am continually praying, but He may not, and in that case would it not be better for me to try and look out for something else? ...
>
> 'THEOBALD PONTIFEX.'

'DEAR THEOBALD, ...

'Of course you needn't be ordained: nobody will compel you; you are perfectly free; you are twenty-three years of age, and should know your own mind; but why not have known it sooner, instead of never so much as breathing a hint of opposition until I have had all the expense of sending you to the University,

which I should never have done unless I had believed you to have
made up your mind about taking orders? I have letters from you
in which you express the most perfect willingness to be
ordained, and your brother and sisters will bear me out in saying
that no pressure of any sort has been put upon you. You mistake
your own mind, and are suffering from a nervous timidity which
may be very natural but may not the less be pregnant with
serious consequences to yourself. I am not at all well, and the
anxiety occasioned by your letter is naturally preying upon me.
May God guide you to a better judgment. – Your affectionate
father.

'G. PONTIFEX.'

On receipt of this letter Theobald plucked up his spirits. 'My
father,' he said to himself, 'tells me I need not be ordained if I do
not like. I do not like, and therefore I will not be ordained. But
what was the meaning of the words "pregnant with serious
consequences to yourself"? Did there lurk a threat under these
words – though it was impossible to lay hold of it or of them?
Were they not intended to produce all the effect of a threat
without being actually threatening?'

Theobald knew his father well enough to be little likely to
misapprehend his meaning, but having ventured so far on the
path of opposition, and being really anxious to get out of being
ordained if he could, he determined to venture farther. He
accordingly wrote the following:

'MY DEAR FATHER. – You tell me – and I heartily thank you – that
no one will compel me to be ordained. I knew you could not
press ordination upon me if my conscience was seriously
opposed to it; I have therefore resolved on giving up the idea,
and believe that if you will continue to allow me what you do at
present, until I get my fellowship, which should not be long, I
will then cease putting you to further expense. I will make up my
mind as soon as possible what profession I will adopt, and will let
you know at once. – Your affectionate son,

'THEOBALD PONTIFEX.'

The remaining letter, written by return of post, must now be
given. It has the merit of brevity.

'DEAR THEOBALD. – I have received yours. I am at a loss to
conceive its motive, but am very clear as to its effect. You shall
not receive a single sixpence from me till you come to your

senses. Should you persist in your folly and wickedness, I am happy to remember that I have got other children whose conduct I can depend upon to be a source of credit and happiness to me. – Your affectionate but troubled father,

'G. PONTIFEX.'

I do not know the immediate sequel to the foregoing correspondence, but it all came perfectly right in the end. Either Theobald's heart failed him, or he interpreted the outward shove which his father gave him as the inward call for which I have no doubt he prayed with great earnestness – for he was a firm believer in the efficacy of prayer ... In the end Theobald got his fellowship by a stroke of luck very soon after taking his degree, and was ordained in the autumn of the same year, 1825.

Samuel Butler (1835–1902), *The Way of All Flesh*, chapter 8.

Prayed and felt for all

Whether one considers explicit corruption, as do Milton and Brontë, or the more insidious self-deception of which Trollope and Butler write, part of the problem would seem to lie in an unrealistic ideal, with too much expected of the clergy. In *The Deserted Village* (1770) Oliver Goldsmith laments the passing of a golden age of rural life. It provoked a hostile response from George Crabbe, who replied with a quite different account of the countryside in *The Village* (1783). A related and recurring English temptation has been to idealize the country parson. Though Goldsmith was the son of such an Anglo-Irish vicar, it is hard not to convict him here of failing to acknowledge a more complex reality.

> Near yonder copse, where once the garden smiled,
> And still where many a garden flower grows wild;
> There, where a few torn shrubs the place disclose,
> The village preacher's modest mansion rose.
> A man he was to all the country dear,
> And passing rich with forty pounds a year;
> Remote from towns he ran his godly race,
> Nor e'er had changed, nor wished to change his place;
> Unskilful he to fawn, or seek for power,
> By doctrines fashioned to the varying hour;
> Far other aims his heart had learned to prize,
> More bent to raise the wretched than to rise.
> His house was known to all the vagrant train,
> He chid their wanderings, but relieved their pain;
> The long remembered beggar was his guest,
> Whose beard descending swept his aged breast;

The ruined spendthrift, now no longer proud,
Claimed kindred there, and had his claims allowed;
The broken soldier, kindly bade to stay,
Sat by his fire, and talked the night away;
Wept o'er his wounds, or tales of sorrow done,
Shouldered his crutch, and showed how fields were won;
Pleased with his guests, the good man learned to glow,
And quite forgot their vices in their woe;
Careless their merits, or their faults to scan,
His pity gave ere charity began.

> Oliver Goldsmith (1728–74), from *The Deserted Village*.

The priest's motherly pain

Elizabeth Jennings speaks here movingly of the priest as 'midwife and as
mother' who through the baked white bread offers 'a way to be reborn'. But
also present is the priest's insistence that, were all the focus to be on him,
the burden would be too great – 'no one could feel such passion'. The
appropriate response to objections based on the quality of a clerical life is
thus to insist that the real focus lies elsewhere – in the 'fruitful, hidden
things'.

After the heaped piles and the cornsheaves waiting
To be collected, gathered into barns,
After all fruits have burst their skins, the sating
    Season cools and turns,
And then I think of something that you said
Of when you held the chalice and the bread.

I spoke of Mass and thought of it as close
To how a season feels which stirs and brings
Fire to the hearth, food to the hungry house
    And strange, uncovered things –
God in a garden then in sheaves of corn
And the white bread a way to be reborn.

I thought of priest as midwife and as mother
Feeling the pain, feeling the pleasure too,
    All opposites together,
Until you said no one could feel such passion
And still preserve the power of consecration.

And it is true. How cool the gold sheaves lie,
Rich without need to ask for any more
Richness. The seed, the simple thing must die
    If only to restore

Our faith in fruitful, hidden things. I see
The wine and bread protect our ecstasy.

Elizabeth Jennings (b. 1926), 'Harvest and Consecration'
from *Song for a Birth or a Death* (1961).

The grand Perhaps

In 'Bishop Blougram's Apology' Browning sets a worldly-wise cleric against an implied interlocutor (he never speaks), who is an idealistic non-believer, young and with no place in society. The bishop's monologue begins with issues of faith and doubt. He admits the existence of doubts, but denies that they should play no part in the clerical vocation. Faith and doubt are two sides of the same coin: even the unbeliever cannot escape his bouts of faith – 'hopes and fears / As old and new as Nature's self ... The grand Perhaps!'. (Through the influence of his reading of Shelley, Browning had himself gone through a period of atheism, and so knew both faith and scepticism from experience.) The poem's other main issue is pragmatism versus the view that 'the aim, if reached or not, makes great the life'. The poem's question is whether the bishop's common-sense adaptation to the world is not lacking in aspirations proper to his profession. Whether he is finally the subtle but dishonest defender of vested interests, or has a realistic appreciation of the complexities of life, Browning leaves the reader to judge.

> See the world
> Such as it is, – you made it not, nor I;
> I mean to take it as it is, – and you,
> Not so you'll take it, – though you get nought else.
> I know the special kind of life I like,
> What suits the most my idiosyncrasy,
> Brings out the best of me and bears me fruit
> In power, peace, pleasantness and length of days.
> I find that positive belief does this
> For me, and unbelief, no whit of this.
> – For you, it does, however? – that, we'll try!
> 'T is clear, I cannot lead my life, at least,
> Induce the world to let me peaceably,
> Without declaring at the outset, 'Friends,
> 'I absolutely and peremptorily
> 'Believe!' – I say, faith is my waking life:
> One sleeps, indeed, and dreams at intervals,
> We know, but waking's the main point with us
> And my provision's for life's waking part.
> Accordingly, I use heart, head and hand
> All day, I build, scheme, study, and make friends;

And when night overtakes me, down I lie,
Sleep, dream a little, and get done with it,
The sooner the better, to begin afresh.
What's midnight doubt before the dayspring's faith?
You, the philosopher, that disbelieve,
That recognize the night, give dreams their weight –
To be consistent you should keep your bed,
Abstain from healthy acts that prove you man,
For fear you drowse perhaps at unawares!
And certainly at night you'll sleep and dream,
Live through the day and bustle as you please.
And so you live to sleep as I to wake,
To unbelieve as I to still believe?
Well, and the common sense o' the world calls you
Bed-ridden, – and its good things come to me.
Its estimation, which is half the fight,
That's the first-cabin comfort I secure:
The next ... but you perceive with half an eye!
Come, come, it's best believing, if we may;
You can't but own that!

Robert Browning (1812–89), from 'Bishop Blougram's Apology'.

In God's good time

R. S. Thomas has worked all his life as a pastor in remote Welsh rural communities. Some find his poetry bleak, but it is inspired by a genuine desire to be ruthlessly honest, both about his environment, and the people he serves (who are frequently portrayed as sullen or mean-spirited). Thomas's country clergy are modest and without pretension. Though they leave no permanent record of their experience, and may even be disregarded by those to whom they minister, yet their honest lives issue in 'sublime words' which God, in ways we may not be able to see, will bring to fruition.

I see them working in old rectories
By the sun's light, by candlelight,
Venerable men, their black cloth
A little dusty, a little green
With holy mildew. And yet their skulls,
Ripening over so many prayers,
Toppled into the same grave
With oafs and yokels. They left no books,
Memorial to their lonely thought
In grey parishes; rather they wrote

On men's hearts and in the minds
Of young children sublime words
Too soon forgotten. God in his time
Or out of time will correct this.

R. S. Thomas (b. 1913), 'The Country Clergy'.

THE EMBRACE OF LOVE

Introduction

In his teaching, Jesus affirmed marriage to be a divinely instituted part of the created order (Mark 10:2–9), and it is this image of two people leaving their respective homes to become 'one flesh' which gives the author of the Epistle to the Ephesians his sustained analogy for Christ's total commitment to his Church: 'Husbands love your wives, even as Christ also loved the church, and gave himself for it' (Eph 5:25). In this passage the normal Greek word for sacrament is used ('mystery' in v. 32). Even so, precisely because of its universal character many Christians have been reluctant to call marriage sacramental. Milton, for example, in his posthumously published *Christian Doctrine*, declares of marriage that, 'inasmuch as it is not an institution peculiar to Christian nations, but common to them all by the universal law of mankind, ... it is not even a religious ceremony, still less a sacrament, but a compact purely civil' (ch. 28). Certainly, only very gradually did marriage in church become the norm, a process which was put in reverse by some of the more Protestant denominations. Nonetheless, the reason for seeing it as a special source of divine grace has often been obvious, even to a lapsed Congregationalist such as D. H. Lawrence who, somewhat surprisingly, used his essay 'A Propos of *Lady Chatterley's Lover*' to speak of Jesus giving 'a new beauty to the permanent sacrament of marriage'. Lawrence sees marriage as the divinely appointed means of 'making one complete body out of two incomplete ones', 'the great way of earthly fulfilment for man and woman'.

In what follows, after introductory pieces on the symbolism of the wedding service, we consider this very issue of whether or not marriage can be viewed as a 'natural sacrament', as something implanted by the creator within the divine order as a means of enabling us to share in his own nature as Love. Spenser evokes all nature in endorsement; though the ambivalent attitude of much of Christian history towards sexuality cannot be denied, there is no shortage of material which might be used in his support. Indeed, so lyrical is Milton in *Paradise Lost* that it is difficult to reconcile what he says there with the non-sacramental view recorded above. However, jostling with this notion of sexuality as a natural symbol of divine love is the related

100

idea of marriage as mystical union, Lawrence's 'making one out of two'. God as Trinity is three persons in one, and in religious mystical experience the claim is made that in marriage individuality is transcended in a comparable way. Shakespeare and Davies are alike concerned to assert this claim of marriage. The section ends with the imagery of marriage transferred to the divine. Following traditional interpretations of the Song of Songs, St John of the Cross does not hesitate to apply sexual metaphors to his mystical identification with Christ, while Dickinson and Donne look forward to our ultimate destiny in heaven as marriage with the Lamb.

Nerves on the day

Samuel Richardson's *Pamela* (1740) was one of the most famous novels of the eighteenth century. It tells how, after numerous attempts at seduction by her master, Pamela, a poor serving girl, eventually becomes his wife. Overcoming his own sensibilities and those of his time about marrying 'beneath his station' he discovers that he is really in love with her. However, as their wedding illustrates, Pamela continues to be utterly deferential to her former master, even curtsying at mention of the ring. (Richardson's tone and attitudes readily lent themselves to parody, an opportunity eagerly seized by Fielding in *Shamela*.)

> My dear master came to me, at entering the chapel, and took my hand, and led me up to the altar. 'Remember, my dear girl,' whispered he, 'and be cheerful.' — 'I am, I will, Sir,' said I; but hardly knew what I said; and so you may believe, when I said to Mrs Jewkes, 'Pray, Mrs Jewkes, don't leave me;' as if I had all confidence in her, and none where it was most due. God forgive me! but I never was so absent in my life, as at first: even till Mr Williams had gone on in the service, so far as to the awful words about '*requiring us, as we shall answer at the dreadful day of judgment*;' and then the solemn words, and my master's whispering, 'Mind this, my dear,' made me start. Said he, still whispering, 'Know *you* any impediment?' I blushed, and said, softly, 'None, Sir, but my great unworthiness.'
>
> Then followed the sweet words, *Wilt thou have this woman to thy wedded wife*, &c. and I began to take heart a little, when my dearest master answered audibly to this question, '*I will*.' But I could only make a curtsey, when they asked me; though I am sure, my *heart* was readier than my *speech*, and answered to every article of *obey, serve, love*, and *honour*.
>
> Mr Peters gave me away, and I said after Mr Williams, as well as I could, as my dear master did, with a much better grace, the

words of betrothment; and the ceremony of the ring passing next, I received the dear favour at his worthy hands, with a most grateful heart; and he told me afterwards, that when he had done saying, *With this ring I thee wed*, &c. I curtsied, and said, 'Thank you, Sir.' Maybe I did; for it was a most grateful part of the service, and my heart was overwhelmed with his goodness, and the tender grace wherewith he performed it. I was very glad the next part was the prayer, and kneeling; for I trembled so, I could hardly stand, betwixt fear and joy.

The joining of our hands, and declaration of our being married, to the few witnesses present; for, reckoning Nan, whose curiosity would not let her stay at the door, there were but Mr Peters, and Mrs Jewkes, and she; the blessing, the psalm, and prayers, and the concluding exhortation, were so many beautiful, welcome, and lovely parts of this divine office, that my heart was delighted with them, and my spirits a little freer.

Thus, my dearest parents, is your happy, thrice happy Pamela, at last married.

Samuel Richardson (1689–1761), Pamela.

Symbol of gain or loss

The Church borrowed the ring as a symbol of fidelity from pagan Rome. White as a symbol of purity ('virginal') is also not unique to Christianity; indeed, in some Eastern religions it is used much more widely, as at funerals to convey the related idea of the triumph of spirit over flesh. Where there has been a difference of stress has been in the degree of permanence and exclusivity demanded of the commitment: it must be as total as God's love for us. Here a contemporary poet, reflecting upon his wife's white wedding dress, finds the meaning of the symbol a continuing reality in their present lives. Mary Tyrone, a character in Eugene O'Neill's *A Long Day's Journey into Night*, is their opposite: at the end of the play she appears in a drugged state, carrying her wedding dress, which for her has become only a sign of the youthful happiness she has lost.

> Virginal, folded, it lies in its box,
> this costly symbol you've decided to sell.
>
> 'I don't think,' you tease, 'I'll need it again.'
> The day you and your mother bought it from Harrods
>
> your purse was stolen in the jostling Tube.
> That evening you were starry-eyed, fed up.

Soon we would swear 'In sickness and in health,'
our mouths dry, voices steady ... Side by side,

we joke while a friend admires the stitching:
'No chance now of your descending the stairs

like Mary Tyrone, dress borne in your arms,
"happy for a time"!' You laugh at my play

with the glum scenario, your face tilted
towards me as when, veiled, you'd reached the altar.
Michael O'Neill (b. 1953), 'Wedding Dress' from *The Stripped
Bed*.

The kind god's sacrament

That desire for a permanent and exclusive commitment, of which the
wedding service and its symbolism speak, is by no means confined to
Christians; it is something for which many, if not most, human beings long.
That explains why within the Christian tradition marriage has often been
regarded as a 'natural' sacrament, as something already built into the
created order, even apart from revelation: we are so made that we desire to
reflect God's love at every level of our being. In this poem, Dick Davis uses
the language of 'sacrament' in precisely this non-exclusive way, by setting
his celebration in Cochin, a cosmopolitan port in the Indian state of Kerala.
Though the native Mar Thoma Church traces its origins to the missionary
work of St Thomas the Apostle, many faiths coexist there. Davis's apparent
indifference to a more precise identification of the divine – his relish even of
the variety of religious traditions which Cochin's history allows him to
invoke – highlights one reason why those who want an exclusivist account of
the Christian sacraments have regarded a sacramental description of marriage with suspicion.

Through high defiles of warehouses that dwarf
With undetermined age the passer-by,
   We walk toward the ancient wharf,
Assailed by smells – sweet, pungent, bitter, dry:

The perfumed plunder of a continent.
To this shore Roman, Moslem, Christian, Jew
   Were gathered by the dense, sharp scent;
Absorbed now in the once-outlandish view

They camped by hills their children would call home.
So in the soil blurred Roman coins are found;

Saint Thomas stepped into the foam
And strode ashore, and blessed the acrid ground;

Jews settled here when Sion was laid waste,
And Arabs edged tall dhows into the bay,
  Dutch burghers felt their northern haste,
Becalmed by slow siestas, ebb away ...

So many faiths and peoples mingle here,
Breathing an air benign with spice and scent,
  That we, though strangers, should not fear
To invoke, in honour of our sacrament,

The sensual, wise genius of this place.
Approach, kind god: bestow your gifts on two,
  Your votaries, of different race
Made one, by love, by marriage, and by you.

Dick Davis (b. 1945), 'Memories of Cochin' from *Seeing the World*.

The echoing woods

Like Davis's poem, Spenser's is an epithalamium, a form classical in origin, a poem sung before the bridal chamber. This helps explain the blending of classical imagery and Christian conviction which occurs in Spenser's poem, written to celebrate his own marriage in 1594. But though Spenser begins with classical allusions, he soon switches to imagery drawn from the Song of Songs with which to describe his beloved, and the poem culminates in the Christian marriage service. Though also a pagan theme, the participation of all nature is used to evoke a God who, as Lord of nature, uses the natural processes of erotic love to deepen the couple's commitment to one another.

Ye learnèd sisters, which have oftentimes	*(the Muses)*
Been to me aiding, others to adorn,	
Whom ye thought worthy of your graceful rhymes,	
That even the greatest did not greatly scorn	
To hear their names sung in your simple lays,	*songs*
But joyèd in their praise;	
And when ye list your own mishaps to mourn,	*wish*
Which death, or love, or fortune's wreck did raise,	
Your string could soon to sadder tenor turn,	
And teach the woods and waters to lament	

Your doleful dreriment: *grief*
Now lay those sorrowful complaints aside,
And having all your heads with garlands crowned,
Help me mine own love's praises to resound,
Ne let the same of any be envide: *envied*
So Orpheus did for his own bride,
So I unto myself alone will sing.
The woods shall to me answer and my echo ring. . . .

Wake now, my love, awake, for it is time;
The rosy Morn long since left
          Tithons' bed,   *(lover of the goddess of dawn)*
All ready to her silver coach to climb,
And Phoebus 'gins to show his glorious head.   *(the Sun)*
Hark how the cheerful birds do chant their lays
And carol of love's praise.
The merry lark her matins sings aloft,
The thrush replies, the mavis descant plays,   *song-thrush*
The ouzel shrills, the ruddock warbles soft;   *blackbird/robin*
So goodly all agree with sweet consent,   *harmony*
To this day's merriment.
Ah, my dear love, why do ye sleep thus long,
When meeter were that ye should now awake,   *more fitting*
T'await the coming of your joyous make,   *mate*
And hearken to the birds' love-learnèd song,
The dewy leaves among.
For they of joy and pleasance to you sing,
That all the woods them answer and their echo ring. . . .

Tell me, ye merchants' daughters, did ye see
So fair a creature in your town before,
So sweet, so lovely, and so mild as she,
Adorned with beauty's grace and virtue's store,
Her goodly eyes like sapphires shining bright,
Her forehead ivory white,
Her cheeks like apples which the sun hath rudded,   *reddened*
Her lips like cherries charming men to bite,
Her breast like to a bowl of cream uncrudded,   *fresh*
Her paps like lilies budded,   *breasts*
Her snowy neck like to a marble tower,
And all her body like a palace fair,
Ascending up with many a stately stair
To honour's seat and chastity's sweet bower.
Why stand ye still ye virgins in amaze,

Upon her so to gaze,
Whiles ye forget your former lay to sing,
To which the woods did answer and your echo ring?

But if ye saw that which no eyes can see,
The inward beauty of her lively sprite,   *living spirit*
Garnished with heavenly gifts of high degree,
Much more then would ye wonder at that sight,
And stand astonished like to those which read   *saw*
Medusa's mazeful head.
There dwells sweet love and constant chastity,
Unspotted faith and comely womanhood,
Regard of honour and mild modesty;
There virtue reigns as queen in royal throne,
And giveth laws alone,
The which the base affections do obey,
And yield their services unto her will;
Ne thought of thing uncomely ever may   *unbecoming*
Thereto approach to tempt her mind to ill.
Had ye once seen these her celestial treasures,
And unrevealèd pleasures,
Then would ye wonder and her praises sing,
That all the woods should answer and your echo ring.

Open the temple gates unto my love,
Open them wide that she may enter in,
And all the posts adorn as doth behove,   *is fitting*
And all the pillars deck with garlands trim,
For to receive this saint with honour due,
That cometh in to you.
With trembling steps and humble reverence
She cometh in before th'Almighty's view.
Of her ye virgins learn obedience,
When so ye come into those holy places,
To humble your proud faces:
Bring her up to th' high altar, that she may
The sacred ceremonies there partake,
The which do endless matrimony make,
And let the roaring organs loudly play
The praises of the Lord in lively notes;
The whiles with hollow throats
The choristers the joyous anthem sing,
That all the woods may answer and their echo ring.

Edmund Spenser (*c.* 1552–99), from *Epithalamion*.

Rites mysterious

Though Milton denied the term 'sacrament' to marriage, because it was a natural and not a revealed ordinance, the idea of marriage he seeks to articulate here draws, even against his will, on the language of sacrament. It is almost as though the symbol of the ring, to which Puritans took such exception (as with the signing of the cross at baptism), has been replaced by sexual intercourse as itself the symbol of love made manifest. That is no doubt why in *The Doctrine and Discipline of Divorce* (ch. 4) he even takes issue with the usual, negative reading of Paul's claim that 'it is better to marry than burn' (1 Cor 7:9). For Milton 'burning' does not mean lust but the positive desire for 'the cheerful society of wedlock' which was present even before the Fall. Theologians had for long debated whether alternative means of procreation had existed in Eden or whether at the very least human desire had been totally under rational control. Milton will have none of this: the desire itself is a gift of God.

> Other rites
> Observing none, but adoration pure
> Which God likes best, into their inmost bower
> Handed they went, and eased the putting off
> These troublesome disguises which we wear;
> Straight side by side were laid, nor turned I ween
> Adam from his fair spouse, nor Eve the rites
> Mysterious of connubial love refused,
> Whatever hypocrites austerely talk
> Of purity and place and innocence,
> Defaming as impure what God declares
> Pure, and commands to some, leaves free to all.
> Our maker bids increase, who bids abstain
> But our destroyer, foe to God and man?
> Hail wedded love, mysterious law, true source
> Of human offspring, sole propriety
> In Paradise of all things common else.
> By thee adulterous lust was driven from men
> Among the bestial herds to range; by thee,
> Founded in reason, loyal, just, and pure,
> Relations dear, and all the charities
> Of father, son, and brother first were known.
> Far be it, that I should write thee sin or blame,
> Or think thee unbefitting holiest place;
> Perpetual fountain of domestic sweets,
> Whose bed is undefiled and chaste pronounced,
> Present, or past, as saints and patriarchs used.

Here Love his golden shafts employs, here lights
His constant lamp, and waves his purple wings,
Reigns here and revels; not in the bought smile
Of harlots, loveless, joyless, unendeared,
Casual fruition, nor in court amours
Mixed dance, or wanton masque, or midnight ball,
Or serenade, which the starved lover sings
To his proud fair, best quitted with disdain.
These lulled by nightingales embracing slept,
And on their naked limbs the flowery roof
Showered roses, which the morn repaired.

John Milton (1608–74), from Paradise Lost, Book IV.

From hallowed bodies bred

In this poem, Hopkins stresses the role of marriage as a reflection of divine love or 'charity'. In opening with the blessing of children, Hopkins reflects the traditional Catholic assumption that any union which deliberately excludes the possibility of such fruitfulness is not a proper marriage. It is an emphasis which in the past has often been used to undervalue the positive enjoyment of sexuality upon which Milton is so insistent.

God with honour hang your head,
Groom, and grace you, bride, your bed
With lissome scions, sweet scions,
Out of hallowed bodies bred.

Each be other's comfort kind:
Deep, deeper than divined,
Divine charity, dear charity,
Fast you ever, fast bind.

Then let the March tread our ears:
I to him turn with tears
Who to wedlock, his wonder wedlock,
Deals triumph and immortal years.

Gerard Manley Hopkins (1844–89), 'At the
Wedding March'.

Using one's instrument night and day

Strong though the linking of sexuality and procreation has been within the Catholic tradition, Milton's notion of enjoying a divine gift is sometimes not far distant. Marriage is a repeated subject of *The Canterbury Tales*, central to the stories of no less than seven pilgrims. In the last of these the Franklin rejects the view that human love has anything to do with 'maistry' or 'regne', the hierarchical rule of husband over wife. Instead, the woman is there able to speak of 'taking a servant when she took a lord'. While the Franklin's Tale shows an ideally harmonious relationship based on careful consideration for each other between the marriage partners, the Wife of Bath's Tale attacks the traditional hierarchy of husband and wife by inverting it. The Wife herself has already had five husbands, and in the Prologue to the story which she offers to her fellow-pilgrims on their way to Becket's shrine at Canterbury we are provided with a comic but robust justification of her attitudes. While accepting the legitimacy of celibacy as an ideal, she notes that its continued existence depends on the married state. Even the celibate Paul conceded that it was 'better to marry than to burn' (1 Cor 7:9). So why not enjoy the obligation on some 'to wax and multiply' (Gen 1:28)?

God bad us for to wax and multiply.	*increase*
That gentle text can I well understand.	*noble*
Eke well I wot be saidë, mine husband	*also/know*
Should lete father and mother, and take me;	*leave/cleave*
But of no number mention made he,	
Of bigamy or of octagamy!	
Why shouldë men speak of it villainy? ...	*reproachfully*
I wot as well as ye, it is no dread,	*doubt*
The apostle, when he speaketh of maidenhead,	
He said, that precept thereof had he none.	
Men may conseille a woman to been oon,	*advise/single*
But conseilling is no commandëment;	*advice*
He put it in our ownë judgement.	
For haddë God commanded maidenhead,	
Then had he damnèd wedding with the deed.	
And certes, if there were no seed y-sow,	*certainly*
Virginity, whereof then should it grow? ...	
Virginity is great perfection,	
And continence eke with devotion.	
But Christ, that of perfection is well,	*wellspring*
Bad not every wight he should go sell	*person*
All that he had, and give it to the poor,	
And in such wise follow him and his fore.	*footsteps*
He spoke to them that would live perfectly;	
And lordings, by your leave, that am not I.	
I will bestow the flower of all mine age	
In the actës and in fruit of marriage.	

Tell me also, to what conclusion   *purpose*
Were members made of generation,   *instruments/procreation*
And of so perfect wise a wight y-wrought?   *manner*
Trusteth right well, they were not made for nought.
Glose whoso will,   *interpret scripture*
     and say both up and down,   *in all respects*
That they were maked for purgation
Of urine, and our bothë thingës small
Were eke to know a female from a male,
And for none other causë: say ye no?
The experience wot well it is not so;   *knows*
So that the clerkës   *providing that/clerics*
     be not with me wroth,   *angry*
I say this, that they maked been for both,
This is to say, for office, and for ease   *to be functional*
Of engendrure, there we not God displease.   *procreation*
Why should men elles in their bookës set,   *otherwise*
That man shall yieldë to his wife her debt?   *pay*
Now wherewith should he make his payement,
If he ne used his sely instrument?   *blessed*
Then were they made upon a creature,
To purge urine, and eke for engendrure.
But I say not that every wight is hold,   *obliged*
That hath such harneys as I to you told,   *equipment*
To go and usen them in engendrure;
Then should men take of chastity no cure.   *care*
Christ was a maid, and shapen as a man,
And many a saint, sith that the world began,   *since*
Yet lived they ever in perfect chastity.
I nil envyë no virginity!   *will not*
Let them be bred of purèd wheatë seed,
And let us wives hoten   *be called*
     barley-bread!   *(an inexpensive bread)*
And yet with barley-bread, Mark tellë can,
Our Lord Jesu refreshèd many a man.
In such estate as God hath clepèd us   *called*
I will persevere, I am not precious.   *fastidious*
In wifehood I will use my instrument
As freely as my maker hath it sent.

Geoffrey Chaucer (*c.* 1343–1400), from 'The Wife of Bath's
Prologue', *The Canterbury Tales*.

Two sexes in one body

In treating sexuality sacramentally, the Christian tradition has had in mind not only the way in which as natural sacrament it can reflect the creator's love, but also its capacity to speak of intimate union, the transcending of individual consciousness of a kind that also occurs both in human religious experience and within God himself. In this poem, Sir John Davies uses pagan mythology as a vehicle for this thought. God has so made us that male and female are fragments of a once unitary being and so an essential complement one to the other, a myth which is found in a number of classical texts, including Plato's *Symposium*. For Davies – whose best known poem, *Orchestra*, celebrates the created world dancing in harmony – this is more than mythology: it reflects the bond of unity which God has imposed on the world as a whole. The mystical language of a John or a Paul is thus already at the heart of human experience.

> When the first man from Paradise was driven
> He did from thence his only comfort bear;
> He still enjoys his wife, which God had given,
> Though he from other joys divorcèd were.
>
> This cordial comfort of society,
> This true-love knot that ties the heart and will,
> When man was in th'extremest misery,
> To keep his heart from breaking rested still.
>
> There is a tale that when the world began
> Both sexes in one body did remain,
> Till Jove, offended with that double man,
> Caused Vulcan to divide him into twain.
>
> In this division he the heart did sever,
> But cunningly he did indent the heart,
> That if they should be reunited ever,
> Each part might know which was the counterpart.
>
> Since then all men and women think it long,
> Till each of them their other part have met;
> Sometimes they meet the right, sometimes the wrong;
> This discontent, and that doth joy beget. ...
>
> And thus the man which Vulcan did divide
> Is now again by Hymen made entire,   *(Greek god of marriage)*
> And all the ruin is re-edified,
> Two being made one by this divine desire.

Sweet marriage is the honey never cloying,
The tune which being still played doth ever please,
The pleasure which is virtue's in enjoying;
It is the band of peace and yoke of ease.

It is a yoke, but sweet and light it is;
The fellowship doth take away the trouble;
For every grief is made half less by this,
And every joy is by reflection double.

It is a band, but one of love's sweet bands,
Such as he binds the world's great parts withal,
Whose wonderous frame by their convention stands,
But being disbanded would to ruin fall.

Sir John Davies (1569–1626), from 'An Elegy in Praise of
Marriage'.

A mutual flame

This poem was written for a volume celebrating the marriage of Sir John
Salisbury and his wife Ursula. Initially it reads more like a poem about death
than life, until one realizes that the two birds which are its subject are, by
convention, symbolic. The turtle-dove symbolizes fidelity, and the phoenix
– a legendary bird which is reborn from its own ashes – immortality. (As
early as the first century [in St Clement's first letter to the Corinthians] this
myth was appropriated by Christianity as a symbol of resurrection.) Shakespeare treats the birds as incarnate forms of ideal qualities: they typify all
truth and beauty. The poem combines a speculative treatment of ideas with
an incantatory mysticism to celebrate the birds' ideal love. They achieved
complete spiritual communion, and in so doing confounded the understandings of ordinary consciousness. They immolated themselves in order
to be joined in love for ever: theirs was a love stronger than death.

Let the bird of loudest lay,   *song*
On the sole Arabian tree,
Herald sad and trumpet be,
To whose sound chaste wings obey.

But thou shrieking harbinger,   *(the owl)*
Foul precurrer of the fiend,   *precursor*
Augur of the fever's end,
To this troop come thou not near!

From this session interdict
Every fowl of tyrant wing,
Save the eagle, feath'red king:
Keep the obsequy so strict.

Let the priest in surplice white,
That defunctive music can,   *funereal*
Be the death-divining swan,
Lest the requiem lack his right.

And thou treble-dated crow,   *long-lived*
That thy sable gender mak'st
With the breath thou giv'st and tak'st,
'Mongst our mourners shalt thou go.

Here the anthem doth commence:
Love and constancy is dead;
Phoenix and the turtle fled
In a mutual flame from hence.

So they loved, as love in twain
Had the essence but in one;
Two distincts, division none:
Number there in love was slain.

Hearts remote, yet not asunder;
Distance, and no space was seen
'Twixt this turtle and his queen:
But in them it were a wonder.

So between them love did shine,
That the turtle saw his right
Flaming in the phoenix' sight;
Either was the other's mine.

Property was thus appalled,
That the self was not the same;
Single nature's double name
Neither two nor one was called.

Reason, in itself confounded,
Saw division grow together,
To themselves yet either neither,
Simple were so well compounded,

That it cried, How true a twain
Seemeth this concordant one!
Love hath reason, reason none,
If what parts can so remain.

Whereupon it made this threne   *funeral song*
To the phoenix and the dove,
Co-supremes and stars of love,
As chorus to their tragic scene.

THRENOS

Beauty, truth, and rarity,
Grace in all simplicity,
Here enclosed, in cinders lie.

Death is now the phoenix' nest;
And the turtle's loyal breast
To eternity doth rest.

Leaving no posterity,
'Twas not their infirmity,
It was married chastity.

Truth may seem, but cannot be;
Beauty brag, but 'tis not she;
Truth and beauty buried be.

To this urn let those repair
That are either true or fair;
For these dead birds sigh a prayer.

William Shakespeare (1564–1616), 'The Phoenix
and the Turtle'.

The divine bridegroom

In earlier extracts, even while talking of the sacramental, the primary focus
has been on the human, whether it be sexuality as an expression of love or
the mystical character of marital union. But it is, of course, possible to
reverse the emphasis, and use the human as a way of illuminating the
divine.

Apart from his own original work, the South African poet Roy Campbell
translated poetry from French, Portuguese and Latin, as well as from
Spanish; he was converted to Roman Catholicism in 1935. His *Poems of St
John of the Cross* appeared in 1951. John (1542–91), together with Teresa of
Avila, was responsible for reforming the Carmelite order. In his poetry he
makes much use of the sexual imagery of the Song of Songs to describe the
soul's marriage to Christ. She is the 'bride' who 'upon a gloomy night'
discovers her 'lover'. Paradoxically the imagery of erotic love is used to
describe a spiritual experience which culminates in the suspension of all
sensuous awareness.

Upon a gloomy night,
With all my cares to loving ardours flushed,
(O venture of delight!)

With nobody in sight
I went abroad when all my house was hushed.

In safety, in disguise,
In darkness up the secret stair I crept,
(O happy enterprise!)
Concealed from other eyes
When all my house at length in silence slept.

Upon that lucky night
In secrecy, inscrutable to sight,
I went without discerning
And with no other light
Except for that which in my heart was burning.

It lit and led me through
More certain than the light of noonday clear
To where One waited near
Whose presence well I knew,
There where no other presence might appear.

Oh night that was my guide!
Oh darkness dearer than the morning's pride,
Oh night that joined the lover
To the beloved bride
Transfiguring them each into the other.

Within my flowering breast
Which only for himself entire I save
He sank into his rest
And all my gifts I gave
Lulled by the airs with which the cedars wave.

Over the ramparts fanned
While the fresh wind was fluttering his tresses,
With his serenest hand
My neck he wounded, and
Suspended every sense with its caresses.

Lost to myself I stayed
My face upon my lover having laid
From all endeavour ceasing:
And all my cares releasing
Threw them amongst the lilies there to fade.

St John of the Cross (1542–91), 'Song of the Soul in
    Rapture', translated by Roy Campbell (1902–57).

The naked sacrament

Apart from imagery drawn from the Song of Songs, the most favoured text
for using marriage to speak directly of divine realities comes from the Book
of Revelation, which speaks of our ultimate destiny as 'the marriage supper
of the Lamb' (Rev 19:9). Here Emily Dickinson envisages herself taking
leave of a dear friend for the last time in this life. As Christ comes naked to
us in the eucharist (without 'wardrobe'), so words on this occasion were
pointless. The friends know they will be carried through suffering ('Cal-
varies of love') to a new and deeper intimacy, 'that new marriage' which lies
beyond the grave.

> There came a day at summer's full
> Entirely for me;
> I thought that such were for the saints
> Where resurrection be.
>
> The sun as common went abroad,
> The flowers accustomed blew,
> As if no soul the solstice passed
> That maketh all things new.
>
> The time was scarce profaned by speech,
> The symbol of a word
> Was needless as at sacrament
> The wardrobe of our Lord.
>
> Each was to each the sealèd church,
> Permitted to commune this time
> Lest we too awkward show
> At supper of the Lamb.
>
> The hours slid fast, as hours will,
> Clutched tight by greedy hands;
> So faces on two decks look back
> Bound to opposing lands.
>
> And so when all the time had leaked,
> Without external sound
> Each bound the other's crucifix –
> We gave no other bond –
>
> Sufficient troth that we shall rise
> (Deposed at length the grave)
> To that new marriage,
> Justified through Calvaries of love.

>   Emily Dickinson (1830–86), *c.* 1861.

Marriage with the Lamb

In this marriage sermon Donne has already discussed two forms of marriage, that of Adam and Eve as the model of all sexual love, and the spiritual marriage in this life of the individual soul to Christ. Now he carries his text ('And I will marry thee unto me for ever') to its logical conclusion in a third and eternal marriage to Christ in the Church triumphant at the end of time. Like Dickinson using the imagery of the marriage supper of the Lamb, Donne sees the soul purified and transformed by that union and prays that the present marriage he is celebrating as a priest may be a 'type' or pattern of what is to come. He thus eloquently expresses the sacramental character of married love as an instrument for bringing us closer to an eternal relationship with the divine.

> In this third marriage the persons are the Lamb and my soul. *The marriage of the Lamb is come, and blessed are they that are called to the marriage supper of the Lamb*, says St John [Rev 19:7, 9], speaking of our state in the general resurrection. That Lamb who was *brought to the slaughter and opened not his mouth* [Isaiah 53:7], and I who have opened my mouth and poured out imprecations and curses upon men, and execrations and blasphemies against God upon every occasion; that Lamb who *was slain from the beginning* [Rev 13:8], and I who was slain by him who *was a murderer from the beginning* [John 8:44]; that Lamb which took away the sins of the world, and I who brought more sins into the world than any sacrifice but the blood of this Lamb could take away: this Lamb and I shall meet and marry. This is not a clandestine marriage, not the private seal of Christ in the obsignation of his Spirit; and yet such a clandestine marriage is a good marriage. Nor it is not such a parish marriage, as when Christ married me to himself at my baptism, in a church here; and yet that marriage of a Christian soul to Christ in that sacrament is a blessed marriage. But this is a marriage in that great and glorious congregation, where all my sins shall be laid open to the eyes of all the world; where all the blessed virgins shall see all my uncleanness, and all the martyrs see all my tergiversations, and all the confessors see all my double dealings in God's cause; where Abraham shall see my faithlessness in God's promises; and Job my impatience in God's corrections; and Lazarus my hardness of heart in distributing to the poor; and those virgins, and martyrs and confessors, and Abraham, and Job, and Lazarus, and all that congregation, shall look upon me, and upon one another, as though they would all forbid those banns, and say to one another, 'Will this Lamb have anything to

do with this soul?' And yet there and then this Lamb shall marry me, and marry me for ever. . . .

I shall see all the beauty, and all the glory of all the saints of God, and love them all, and know that the Lamb loves them too, without jealousy, on his part, or theirs, or mine, and so be married for ever, without interruption, or diminution, or change of affection. I shall see the sun black as sackcloth of hair, and the moon become as blood, and the stars fall as a figtree casts her untimely figs, and the heavens rolled up together as a scroll [Rev 6:12–14]. I shall see a divorce between princes and their prerogatives, between nature and all her elements, between the spheres and all their intelligences, between matter itself and all her forms, and my marriage shall be for ever. I shall see an end of faith, nothing to be believed that I do not know; and an end of hope, nothing to be wished that I do not enjoy; but no end of that love in which I am married to the Lamb for ever. Yea, I shall see an end of some of the offices of the Lamb himself; Christ himself shall be no longer a mediator, an intercessor, an advocate, and yet shall continue a husband to my soul for ever. Where I shall be rich enough without jointure, for my husband cannot die; and wise enough without experience, for no new thing can happen there; and healthy enough without physic, for no sickness can enter; and (which is by much the highest of all) safe enough without grace, for no temptation that needs particular grace can attempt me. There, where the angels, which cannot die, could not live, this very body which cannot choose but die, shall live, and live as long as that God of life that made it. Lighten our darkness, we beseech thee, O Lord, that in thy light we may see light. Illustrate our understandings, kindle our affections, pour oil to our zeal, that we may come to the marriage of this Lamb, and that this Lamb may come quickly to this marriage. And in the meantime bless these thy servants, with making this secular marriage a type of the spiritual, and the spiritual an earnest of that eternal, which they and we, by thy mercy, shall have in the kingdom which thy Son our Saviour hath purchased with the inestimable price of his incorruptible blood.

John Donne (1572–1631), from a marriage sermon of 1621 on Hosea 2:19.

GRACED PRESENCES

Introduction

In the two previous sections we considered two specific ways in which human beings can act sacramentally, the role of the priest and that of the married couple. Scripture, however, claims that we are all made in the divine image (Gen 1:26–27), and not just those who fall into these two categories; so it must be possible for us all to some degree, however small, to participate in and reflect divine qualities. The extracts from Blake, Dante and Thompson with which we begin may seem too sanguine for those convinced of the extent of human depravity and original sin. But, however strongly such a view is held, must not some possibility of 'a graced presence' enabling a sacramental disclosure of the divine through others be accepted?

For many, the first experience of such graced presences will be in the home, whether this is explicitly Christian or not. It is there that we normally learn the meaning of love, and so are drawn out of ourselves into something larger, which is itself a reflection of the divine love. Despite their different religious backgrounds, Burns and Mahon share this same idea. The most obvious ritual of the home is the meal. Here W. H. Auden develops its sacramental implications. Fast food and television suppers mean that it no longer exercises the dominant role it once did. Even so, it still remains a primary vehicle of social exchange, for cementing friendships. It thus retains its symbolic role of relating us more effectively one to another, and reflects and reinforces the principal Christian symbolic act: not only did the eucharist take its origins from a meal, it too is concerned with deepening personal relations, in this case with Christ.

Yet, it is not only the love and personal relations which characterize God that one human being can mediate to another: this is also true of divine creativity. Human creativity in art (Thomas, Jennings) and music (Gascoyne), whatever the intention of the artist concerned, can speak of the divine artist from whom that creativity has ultimately derived. This applies not only to the plastic arts, and to music, but also to literature. The beauty of the poetry and prose in this volume can thus equally act sacramentally, pointing beyond itself to the beauty of the divine. God's love, intelligibility and grandeur are thus disclosed in and through the writer's art.

119

God in every human form

In this early poem Blake asserts the presence of the divine image in all human beings, and the consequent necessity of respecting people, whatever their religious commitment ('Turk' is here used as a synonym for 'Muslim'). In a more exclusively Christian context love as 'the human form divine' might most naturally refer to Christ. But at this stage Blake saw all religions as equally valid refractions of the divine, and in this poem he implies that anyone is most like God when love and compassion are shown.

> To Mercy, Pity, Peace and Love
> All pray in their distress,
> And to these virtues of delight
> Return their thankfulness.
>
> For Mercy, Pity, Peace and Love
> Is God our father dear,
> And Mercy, Pity, Peace and Love
> Is Man his child and care.
>
> For Mercy has a human heart,
> Pity a human face,
> And Love the human form divine,
> And Peace the human dress.
>
> Then every man of every clime
> That prays in his distress,
> Prays to the human form divine:
> Love, Mercy, Pity, Peace.
>
> And all must love the human form,
> In heathen, Turk or Jew.
> Where Mercy, Love and Pity dwell,
> There God is dwelling too.

> William Blake (1757–1827), 'The Divine
> Image' from *Songs of Innocence* (1789).

Love's salutation

The son of a Neapolitan political exile, and with Dante in his name, it was perhaps inevitable that Rossetti should take an interest in his more famous namesake. Though the medieval Dante was married with at least four children, it was the noble Florentine woman Beatrice Portinari who, he believed, drew out of him all that was noblest. Beatrice died in 1290, and two years later Dante began *La Vita Nuova* as a way of trying to give expression to his love for her. He insists that it was through her that the highest form of human love (which in his case clearly included an element of sublimated sexual feeling) became possible for him. As he puts it here, his love for Beatrice meant that 'there was no man mine enemy any longer'. It is because of this overwhelming and purifying love that it is Beatrice who leads Dante from the highest levels of Purgatory to the final vision of God in *The Divine Comedy*. Rossetti produced his translation of *La Vita Nuova* while in love with the beautiful Elizabeth Siddal, whom he married in 1860, the year before the translation was published.

> Here it is fitting for me to depart a little from this present matter, that it may be rightly understood of what surpassing virtue her salutation was to me. To the which end I say that when she appeared in any place, it seemed to me, by the hope of her excellent salutation, that there was no man mine enemy any longer; and such warmth of charity came upon me that most certainly in that moment I would have pardoned whosoever had done me an injury; and if one should then have questioned me concerning any matter, I could only have said unto him 'Love,' with a countenance clothed in humbleness. And what time she made ready to salute me, the spirit of Love, destroying all other perceptions, thrust forth the feeble spirits of my eyes, saying, 'Do homage unto your mistress,' and putting itself in their place to obey: so that he who would, might then have beheld Love, beholding the lids of mine eyes shake. And when this most gentle lady gave her salutation, Love, so far from being a medium beclouding mine intolerable beatitude, then bred in me such an overpowering sweetness that my body, being all subjected thereto, remained many times helpless and passive. Whereby it is made manifest that in her salutation alone was there any beatitude for me, which then very often went beyond my endurance.

> Dante Alighieri (1265–1321), from *La Vita Nuova*, translated by Dante Gabriel Rossetti (1828–82).

Betwixt heaven and Charing Cross

Educated at Ushaw seminary near Durham, Francis Thompson had been intended for the priesthood, but was judged unsuitable. Falling prey to opium addiction, he was rescued from destitution by the poet Alice Meynell, but she was unable to prevent the drug eventually taking its toll in his early death. In this, perhaps his most famous poem, he takes as his starting point traditional Catholic theology, that the angels are everywhere about us in 'their ancient places', including, of course, our guardian angels (Matt 18:10). Were we alive to the divine all about us, we also could have an experience like Jacob's at Bethel (Gen 28:12–17), but with this difference: we will find God in the heart of the city, amid the 'traffic' of people in Charing Cross and on the Thames. In other words, God is disclosed here sacramentally through people rather than through the images of nature, with which the poem begins.

> O world invisible, we view thee,
> O world intangible, we touch thee,
> O world unknowable, we know thee,
> Inapprehensible, we clutch thee!
>
> Does the fish soar to find the ocean,
> The eagle plunge to find the air –
> That we ask of the stars in motion
> If they have rumour of thee there?
>
> Not where the wheeling systems darken,
> And our benumbed conceiving soars! –
> The drift of pinions, would we hearken,
> Beats at our own clay-shuttered doors.
>
> The angels keep their ancient places; –
> Turn but a stone, and start a wing!
> 'Tis ye, 'tis your estrangèd faces,
> That miss the many-splendoured thing.
>
> But (when so sad thou canst not sadder)
> Cry; – and upon thy so sore loss
> Shall shine the traffic of Jacob's ladder
> Pitched betwixt heaven and Charing Cross.
>
> Yea, in the night, my Soul, my daughter,
> Cry, – clinging Heaven by the hems;
> And lo, Christ walking on the water,
> Not of Genesereth, but Thames!
>
> Francis Thompson (1859–1907).

Priest of home and hearth

Our most basic experience of other people often comes in the home. This poem is commonly taken to be a tribute to the humble home in which Burns himself was brought up in Ayrshire. Still surviving is a 'Manual of Religious Belief' which his father wrote, and certainly his father took considerable pains to secure his children's education, even if he seems to have moved from one unsuccessful farm to another. It is a home in which love and mutual concern reign. Significantly, not only is a large portion of the poem given over to the family's Bible reading and prayers, Burns gives this an explicitly sacramental character. The father is called 'priest-like' in the performance of his task, and with this happy scene is contrasted 'poor Religion's pride' with its 'sacerdotal stole' (in Catholic churches the scarf that is the sign of the priestly function). The father is a 'priest' not only in conveying the truths of the Bible, but also in mediating the divine love in the love which characterizes his own home.

> My loved, my honoured, much respected friend!
>   No mercenary bard his homage pays;
> With honest pride, I scorn each selfish end,
>   My dearest meed, a friend's esteem and praise:
>   To you I sing, in simple Scottish lays,
> The lowly train in life's sequestered scene;
>   The native feelings strong, the guileless ways;
> What Aiken in a cottage would have been;
> Ah! tho' his worth unknown, far happier there I ween!

> November chill blaws loud wi' angry sugh;   *wail*
>   The short'ning winter-day is near a close;
> The miry beasts retreating frae the pleugh;   *plough*
>   The black'ning trains o' craws to their repose:
>   The toil-worn Cotter frae his labour goes –
> This night his weekly moil is at an end,
>   Collects his spades, his mattocks, and his hoes,
> Hoping the morn in ease and rest to spend,
> And weary, o'er the moor, his course does hameward bend.

> At length his lonely cot appears in view,
>   Beneath the shelter of an agèd tree;
> Th' expectant wee-things, toddlin, stacher through   *totter*
>   To meet their dad, wi' flichterin' noise and glee.   *fluttering*
>   His wee bit ingle, blinkin bonilie,
> His clean hearth-stane, his thrifty wifie's smile,
>   The lisping infant, prattling on his knee,
> Does a' his weary carking cares beguile,   *anxious*
> And makes him quite forget his labour and his toil. ...

> The chearfu' supper done, wi' serious face,
>   They, round the ingle, form a circle wide;
> The sire turns o'er, wi' patriarchal grace,
>   The big ha'-Bible, ance his father's pride.
>   His bonnet rev'rently is laid aside,
> His lyart haffets wearing thin and bare;   *grey side-locks*
>   Those strains that once did sweet in Zion glide,

He wales a portion with judicious care,   *selects*
And 'Let us worship God!' he says, with solemn air.

They chant their artless notes in simple guise,
    They tune their hearts, by far the noblest aim;
Perhaps *Dundee's* wild-warbling measures rise,
    Or plaintive *Martyrs*, worthy of the name;
    Or noble *Elgin* beets the heaven-ward flame,   *fans*
The sweetest far of Scotia's holy lays:
    Compared with these, Italian trills are tame;
The tickled ears no heart-felt raptures raise;
Nae unison hae they, with our Creator's praise.

The priest-like father reads the sacred page,
    How Abram was the friend of God on high;
Or, Moses bade eternal warfare wage
    With Amalek's ungracious progeny;
    Or, how the royal Bard did groaning lie
Beneath the stroke of Heaven's avenging ire;
    Or Job's pathetic plaint, and wailing cry;
Or rapt Isaiah's wild, seraphic fire;
Or other holy Seers that tune the sacred lyre.

Perhaps the Christian volume is the theme:
    How guiltless blood for guilty man was shed;
How He, who bore in Heaven the second name,
    Had not on earth whereon to lay His head;
    How His first followers and servants sped;
The precepts sage they wrote to many a land:
    How he, who lone in Patmos banishèd,
Saw in the sun a mighty angel stand,
And heard great Bab'lon's doom pronounced by Heaven's
        command.

Then kneeling down to Heaven's Eternal King,
    The saint, the father, and the husband prays:
Hope 'springs exulting on triumphant wing'
    That thus they all shall meet in future days,
    There, ever bask in uncreated rays,
No more to sigh or shed the bitter tear,
    Together hymning their Creator's praise,
In such society, yet still more dear;
While circling Time moves round in an eternal sphere.

Compared with this, how poor Religion's pride,
    In all the pomp of method, and of art;

When men display to congregations wide
  Devotion's ev'ry grace, except the heart!
The Power, incensed, the pageant will desert,
The pompous strain, the sacerdotal stole:
  But haply, in some cottage far apart,
May hear, well-pleased, the language of the soul,
And in His Book of Life the inmates poor enroll.

Robert Burns (1759–96), from 'The Cotter's Saturday Night'.

The godly glow from the petrol pump

The Irish poet Derek Mahon reflects upon a very different sort of home, an improvised former garage, from which the occupants eventually sought escape through emigration, perhaps to England or the United States. Yet it was still a home, and as such has a certain sanctity. Even as what remains returns to its natural state, it still 'shines with a late sacramental gleam'. To reinforce the point, Mahon turns to classical mythology. The petrol pumps recall the devoted elderly couple, Philemon and Baucis, who at their own request were turned into trees with boughs intertwined, after having entertained Zeus and Hermes unawares when wealthier homes had turned them away.

    Surely you paused at this roadside oasis
    In your nomadic youth, and saw the mound
    Of never-used cement, the curious faces,
    The soft-drink ads and the uneven ground
    Rainbowed with oily puddles, where a snail
    Had scrawled its slimy, phosphorescent trail.

    Like a frontier store-front in an old western
    It might have nothing behind it but thin air,
    Building materials, fruit boxes, scrap iron,
    Dust-laden shrubs and coils of rusty wire,
    A cabbage-white fluttering in the sodden
    Silence of an untended kitchen garden.

    Nirvana! But the cracked panes reveal a dark
    Interior echoing with the cries of children.
    Here in this quiet corner of Co. Cork
    A family ate, slept, and watched the rain
    Dance clean and cobalt the exhausted grit
    So that the mind shrank from the glare of it.

    Where did they go? South Boston? Cricklewood?
    Somebody somewhere thinks of this as home,

Remembering the old pumps where they stood,
Antique now, squirting juice into a chrome
Lagonda or a dung-caked tractor while
A cloud swam on a cloud-reflecting tile.

Surely a whitewashed sun-trap at the back
Gave way to hens, wild thyme, and the first few
Shadowy yards of an overgrown cart-track,
Tyres in the branches such as Noah knew –
Beyond, a swoop of mountain where you heard,
Disconsolate in the haze, a single blackbird.

Left to itself, the functional will cast
A death-bed glow of picturesque abandon.
The intact antiquities of the recent past,
Dropped from the retail catalogues, return
To the materials that gave rise to them
And shine with a late sacramental gleam.

A god who spent the night here once rewarded
Natural courtesy with eternal life –
Changing to petrol pumps, that they be spared
For ever there, an old man and his wife.
The virgin who escaped his dark design
Sanctions the townland from her prickly shrine.

We might be anywhere – in the Dordogne,
Iquitos, Bethlehem – wherever the force
Of gravity secures houses and the sun
Selects this fan-blade of the universe
Decelerating while the fates devise
What outcome for the dawdling galaxies?

But we are in one place and one place only,
One of the milestones of earth-residence
Unique in each particular, the thinly
Peopled hinterland serenely tense –
Not in the hope of a resplendent future
But with a sure sense of its intrinsic nature.

Derek Mahon (b. 1941), 'A Garage in Co. Cork' from *The
Hunt by Night*.

At God's board

This is part of a collection on the theme of the home in which Auden several
times takes up sacramental themes. In this poem, as in 'The Cotter's
Saturday Night', the meal is the primary focus. Amidst the humour over

appropriate numbers at the dinner table and the right behaviour of guests, Auden makes some serious points, not least the sacred and ritual character of eating together. Certain rules of hospitality will contine to apply to 'the sacral dining area' till all things have their end in the feast of Leviathan, the traditional monster whom God will destroy in the last days (Isa 27:1). In the meantime, because 'brains evolved after bowels', we need to get our priorities right. A reverential swallowing of the sumptuous ('dapatical') fare acknowledges the 'grace of Spirit' with which the meal has been prepared; words of appreciation repeat the silent enjoyment. That Auden uses the eucharistic word 're-present', a Hebrew word for eternal ('olamic'), and speaks of 'a sign act' all implies that he takes the meal itself to be sacramental.

> The life of plants
>   is one continuous solitary meal,
>   and ruminants
> hardly interrupt theirs to sleep or to mate, but most
>   predators feel
> ravenous most of the time and competitive
> always, bolting such morsels as they can contrive
> to snatch from the more terrified: pack-hunters do
>   dine *en famille*, it is true,
> with protocol and placement, but none of them play host
>   to a stranger whom they help first. Only man,
>   supererogatory beast,
>   Dame Kind's thoroughbred lunatic, can
>   do the honors of a feast,
>
>   and was doing so
> before the last Glaciation when he offered
>   mammoth-marrow
> and, perhaps, Long Pig, will continue till Doomsday
>   when at God's board
> the saints chew pickled Leviathan. In this age farms
> are no longer crenellated, only cops port arms,
> but the Law of the Hearth is unchanged: a brawler may not
>   be put to death on the spot,
> but he is asked to quit the sacral dining area
>   *instanter*, and a foul-mouth gets the cold
>   shoulder. The right of a guest
> to standing and foster is as old
>   as the ban on incest.
>
>   For authentic
> comity the gathering should be small

and unpublic:
at mass banquets where flosculent speeches are made
        in some hired hall
we think of ourselves or nothing. Christ's cenacle
seated a baker's dozen, King Arthur's rundle
the same, but today, when one's host may well be his own
        chef, servitor and scullion,
when the cost of space can double in a decade,
    even that holy Zodiac number is
        too large a frequency for us:
    in fact, six lenient semble sieges,
            none of them perilous,

        is now a Perfect
    Social Number. But a dinner party,
            however select,
is a worldly rite that nicknames or endearments
            or family
diminutives would profane: two doters who wish
to tiddle and curmurr between the soup and fish
belong in restaurants, all children should be fed
        earlier and be safely in bed.
Well-liking, though, is a must: married maltalents
    engaged in some covert contrast can spoil
        an evening like the glance
    of a single failure in the toil
            of his bosom grievance.

        Not that a god,
    immune to grief, would be an ideal guest:
            he would be too odd
to talk to and, despite his imposing presence, a bore,
            for the funniest
mortals and the kindest are those who are most aware
of the baffle of being, don't kid themselves our care
is consolable, but believe a laugh is less
        heartless than tears, that a hostess
prefers it. Brains evolved after bowels, therefore,
    great assets as fine raiment and good looks
        can be on festive occasions,
    they are not essential like artful cooks
            and stalwart digestions.

I see a table
   at which the youngest and oldest present
      keep the eye grateful
for what Nature's bounty and grace of Spirit can create:
      for the ear's content
one raconteur, one gnostic with amazing shop,
both in a talkative mood but knowing when to stop,
and one wide-traveled worldling to interject now and then
      a sardonic comment, men
and women who enjoy the cloop of corks, appreciate
   dapatical fare, yet can see in swallowing
      a sign act of reverence,
   in speech a work of re-presenting
      the true olamic silence.

W. H. Auden (1907–73), 'Tonight at Seven-thirty' from *Thanksgiving for a Habitat*, X.

Friends not by bread

In this extract from Blake's long poem *Jerusalem* (not to be confused with the more famous lyric which appears at the beginning of his *Milton*), the poet launches an attack on the entire system of sacramental rituals as conceived by the church. His preference is clearly for 'spiritual gifts' over 'corporeal'. Yet ironically he rehabilitates the idea of sacramentality outside the context of formal ritual when he insists that we 'see the Divinity in his children', itself a physical mediation of the divine.

Go, tell them that the worship of God is honouring his gifts
In other men, and loving the greatest men best, each
      according
To his genius, which is the Holy Ghost in Man. There is no
      other
God than that God who is the intellectual fountain of
      humanity.
He who envies or calumniates, which is murder and cruelty,
Murders the Holy One. Go, tell them this and overthrow their
      cup,
Their bread, their altar table, their incense and their oath,
Their marriage and their baptism, their burial and
      consecration.
I have tried to make friends by corporeal gifts but have only
Made enemies; I never made friends but by spiritual gifts,
By severe contentions of friendship and the burning fire of
      thought.
He who would see the Divinity must see him in his children:

One first, in friendship and love; then a divine family; and in
    the midst
Jesus will appear.

William Blake (1757–1827), from Jerusalem, chapter 4.

Art as religion's flower

If the everyday actions of people in the home and at meals can be said to communicate a sense of the divine, may God's presence not be still more powerfully felt in those areas of life where humanity is at its most creative, in art and music? Some thought such as this may help explain why in this poem R. S. Thomas takes almost the exact opposite stance to Blake's towards the rich suggestiveness of ecclesiastical tradition. For Thomas a Protestant insistence on plainness – of ritual, language and adornment – is destructive of positive religious feeling. Worship should properly involve the whole being, emotional and imaginative as well as intellectual. As our physicality enjoins us to fall to our knees in repentance, so our renewal needs material signs like the flowers of spring, or a beautified church. Art is thus not incidental to religion; appropriate symbols are indispensable.

Instead of the altar
the pulpit. Instead
of the bread the fraction
of the language. And God
a shadow of himself
on a blank wall. Their prayers
are a passing of hands
over their brows as though
in an effort to wipe sin
off. Their buildings
are in praise of concrete
and macadam. Frowning
upon divorce, they divorce
art and religion.
Ah, if one flower
had been allowed to grow
between the wall
and the railings as sacrament
of renewal. Instead
two cypresses ail
there, emaciated as the bodies
of the thieves upon Calvary
but with no Saviour between them.

R. S. Thomas (b. 1913), from 'Bleak Liturgies'.

Under the paint

The Welsh poet and artist David Jones, to whom this poem is dedicated, became a convert to Roman Catholicism in 1921. In the same year he began studying art with Eric Gill at Ditchling in Sussex, a community devoted to the sacramentality of work and to promoting a religious attitude to art and craftsmanship. Jones shared with Gill many of his ideas of the artist's role. In this poem Elizabeth Jennings ends by referring to one of those ideas, the notion of art as sacramental. But she begins with an evocation of the natural world. Prompted by the creatively open, calm state that the beautiful natural and artistic surroundings induce, she sees the truth of Jones's view: art points beyond itself to the ultimate Creator no less than does the more explicit bread and wine.

> Window upon the wall, a balcony
> With a light chair, the air and water so
> Mingled you could not say which was the sun
> And which the adamant yet tranquil spray.
> But nothing was confused and nothing slow:
> Each way you looked, always the sea, the sea.
>
> And every shyness that we brought with us
> Was drawn into the pictures on the walls.
> It was so good to sit quite still and lose
> Necessity of discourse, words to choose
> And wonder which were honest and which false.
>
> Then I remembered words that you had said
> Of art as gesture and as sacrament,
> A mountain under the calm form of paint
> Much like the Presence under wine and bread –
> Art with its largesse and its own restraint.

Elizabeth Jennings (b.1926), 'Visit to an Artist' from *Song for a Birth or a Death* (1961).

The music of the skies

David Gascoyne received part of his education at Salisbury Cathedral School. He translated many of the French Surrealist writings, in which, under the influence of Freud's theory of the unconscious, the argument is that we should give free rein to our thoughts and resist logical restraint as narrowing. Gascoyne himself has experimented with disrupting normal patterns of coherence and argument, but in the present poem the mystery of spiritual experience which it is 'beyond our speech / To tell' is suggested only by the opening's inconclusive grammatical structure. Within this, however, an implied argument is fairly easy to follow. The *Sursum Corda* is that point in the liturgy when the priest invites the people to 'Lift up your hearts'. Gascoyne reflects on the power of music to effect exactly that. It clarifies perception, prepares the feelings for the quasi-religious experience of art, and, with its *sostenuto* (sustained playing), discloses 'the sostenuto of the sky', the spiritual which is both within this world and beyond.

> Filters the sunlight from the knife-bright wind
> And rarifies the rumour-burdened air,
> The heart's receptive chalice in pure hands upheld
> Towards the sostenuto of the sky
>
> Supernal voices flood the ear of clay
> And transpierce the dense skull: Reveal
> The immaterial world concealed
> By mortal deafness and the screen of sense,
>
> World of transparency and last release
> And world within the world. Beyond our speech
> To tell what equinoxes of the infinite
> The spirit ranges in its rare utmost flight.

David Gascoyne (b. 1916), 'Mozart: Sursum Corda' from *Miserere and Other Poems* (1937–42).

Seeing nature with God's eyes

Son of an artist and a nun, Filippo Lippi probably studied under Botticelli, and certainly became a Carmelite monk. His most famous painting, 'The Vision of St Bernard', shows a lyrical mysticism, but, taking his cue from a comment by Vasari in his *Lives of the Painters*, Browning gives Lippi a lively monologue in which he expresses discontent with the conventions of the day, which expected art to aim for a spirituality which bypasses the material world. Being brought up in poverty trained Lippi to observe sharply and interpret what he saw: it taught him 'the value and significance of flesh'. Through his art, therefore, he hopes both to act as a medium for disclosing God within the natural world, and to be a vehicle for higher truths normally reserved for the pulpit.

> You're my man, you've seen the world
> – The beauty and the wonder and the power,

The shapes of things, their colours, lights and shades,
Changes, surprises, – and God made it all!
– For what? Do you feel thankful, ay or no,
For this fair town's face, yonder river's line,
The mountain round it and the sky above,
Much more the figures of man, woman, child,
These are the frame to? What's it all about?
To be passed over, despised? or dwelt upon,
Wondered at? oh, this last of course! – you say.
But why not do as well as say, – paint these
Just as they are, careless what comes of it?
God's works – paint anyone, and count it crime
To let a truth slip. Don't object, 'His works
'Are here already; nature is complete:
'Suppose you reproduce her – (which you can't)
There's no advantage! you must beat her, then.'
For, don't you mark? we're made so that we love
First when we see them painted, things we have passed
Perhaps a hundred times nor cared to see;
And so they are better, painted – better to us,
Which is the same thing. Art was given for that;
God uses us to help each other so,
Lending our minds out. Have you noticed, now,
Your cullion's hanging face? A bit of chalk,
And trust me but you should, though! How much more,
If I drew higher things with the same truth!
That were to take the Prior's pulpit-place,
Interpret God to all of you! Oh, oh,
It makes me mad to see what men shall do
And we in our graves! This world's no blot for us,
Nor blank; it means intensely, and means good:
To find its meaning is my meat and drink.

        Robert Browning (1812–89), from 'Fra Lippo Lippi'.

THE BALM OF FORGIVENESS

Introduction

Human penitence and divine forgiveness have always played key interactive roles in the Christian religion. It is a stress which was inherited from Judaism: 'I said, "I will confess my transgressions to the Lord"; then thou didst forgive the guilt of my sin' (Psalm 32:5). In this way God showed his grace or 'goodly favour' towards the penitent in offering the possibility of a fresh start. But grace is of course not necessarily sacramental. What makes it so is when such grace is mediated through some material feature of our world. In the Jewish case one may interpret in this way the concrete sin offerings which the Law required (Lev 1 – 7) and which culminated in the ritual of the Day of Atonement (Lev 16).

In the New Testament, however, these rituals were abolished through being caught up in the significance of Christ's death (e.g. Heb 9), but the notion of sacramental mediation continued, most obviously in the claim now of the Church to mediate such grace (cf. John 20:23). Initially, this appears to have taken an exclusively corporate and public form and to have been particularly associated with the discipline of Lent, but gradually auricular confession developed, the practice of private confession 'to the ear' of a priest. Even so, the legitimacy of confession to those who were not priests was accepted in the East as late as the fourteenth century. In the West, Albert the Great (d. 1280), the teacher of Thomas Aquinas, argued that confession to a lay person had a true sacramental character, while Aquinas himself drew an analogy with lay baptism.

The extracts which follow begin by setting the scene, in terms of the human longing for forgiveness (e.g. Campion) and the way in which God responds by setting no limits to such forgiveness (e.g. Heaney). James Joyce illustrates the character the rite had acquired prior to the Second Vatican Council (1962–65), while Carol Ann Duffy highlights some of its most obvious inadequacies, among them a routine listing of sins rather than a proper concern for the penitent's spiritual development – though William Dunbar's poem refutes the charge that the Middle Ages was unconcerned with serious self-examination. Burns's Holy Willie suggests how much genuine self-examination before God may depend upon the mediation of another: with a listener whose responses we cannot control self-deception is more difficult. Flannery O'Connor rightly observes that what is disclosed remains in God's hands, not ours. While not discounting the importance and legitimacy of confession before a priest, the final group of extracts considers the wider notion of such sacramental mediation. Hawthorne describes a priest mediating grace to a New England 'heretic' despite himself. Spenser stresses the role of the Church as whole; Shakespeare the role of a particular individual; Coleridge that even the non-human creation can mediate grace and so initiate repentance and forgiveness.

Out of my soul's depth

In this free translation of Psalm 130, one of the traditional seven penitential psalms (of which Psalm 51 is the best known), Thomas Campion expresses both the penitent's longing for forgiveness and the resultant experience of divine grace as a generosity out of all proportion to the severity of the fault.

> Out of my soul's depth to thee my cries have sounded:
> Let thine ears my plaints receive, on just fear grounded.
> Lord, should'st thou weigh our faults, who's not confounded?
>
> But with grace thou censur'st thine when they have erred,
> Therefore shall thy blessed name be loved and feared.
> E'en to thy throne my thoughts and eyes are reared.
>
> Thee alone my hopes attend, on thee relying;
> In thy sacred word I'll trust, to thee fast flying,
> Long ere the watch shall break, the morn descrying.
>
> In the mercies of our God who live secured,
> May of full redemption rest in him assured,
> Their sin-sick souls by him shall be recured.

Thomas Campion (1567–1620), from *Two Books of Airs* (*c.* 1613).

An oozing sore

Campion's poem makes no reference to sacramental confession. The sense of release which it can bring is well illustrated by this extract from Joyce's *A Portrait of the Artist as a Young Man*. A semi-autobiographical novel, it describes the development of Stephen Daedalus from childhood to early manhood. As a pupil at a Jesuit school Stephen frequently goes to brothels in the red-light district of Dublin. Terrified into disgust at his sexual sins by a vividly detailed sermon on the punishments of hell, which he hears during an Easter retreat, Stephen goes to confession. Joyce here enters fully into

Stephen's self-disgust and repentance, but by the end of the novel Stephen regards Catholicism as one of the traps which, for the sake of his freedom as an artist, he has to escape. Though understandable in this case, the concentration on sexual sin has often been identified as one of the main reasons for the collapse of auricular confession in the modern world. Roman Catholic practice has been revolutionized since the Second Vatican Council: in what is now known as 'the sacrament of reconciliation', the stress falls more on advice and encouragement than the simple listing of sins.

He was next. He stood up in terror and walked blindly into the box.

At last it had come. He knelt in the silent gloom and raised his eyes to the white crucifix suspended above him. God could see that he was sorry. He would tell all his sins. His confession would be long, long. Everybody in the chapel would know then what a sinner he had been. Let them know. It was true. But God had promised to forgive him if he was sorry. He was sorry. He clasped his hands and raised them towards the white form, praying with darkened eyes, praying with all his trembling body, swaying his head to and fro like a lost creature, praying with whimpering lips.

– Sorry! Sorry! O sorry!

The slide clicked back and his heart bounded in his breast. The face of an old priest was at the grating, averted from him, leaning upon a hand. He made the sign of the cross and prayed of the priest to bless him for he had sinned. Then, bowing his head, he repeated the *Confiteor* in fright. At the words *my most grievous fault* he ceased, breathless.

– How long is it since your last confession, my child?
– A long time, father.
– A month, my child?
– Longer, father.
– Three months, my child?
– Longer, father.
– Six months?
– Eight months, father.

He had begun. The priest asked:

– And what do you remember since that time?

He began to confess his sins: masses missed, prayers not said, lies.

– Anything else, my child?

Sins of anger, envy of others, gluttony, vanity, disobedience.

– Anything else, my child?

– Sloth.

– Anything else, my child?

There was no help. He murmured:

– I ... committed sins of impurity, father.

The priest did not turn his head.

– With yourself, my child?

– And ... with others.

– With women, my child?

– Yes, father.

– Were they married women, my child?

He did not know. His sins trickled from his lips, one by one, trickled in shameful drops from his soul festering and oozing like a sore, a squalid stream of vice. The last sins oozed forth, sluggish, filthy. There was no more to tell. He bowed his head, overcome.

The priest was silent. Then he asked:

– How old are you, my child?

– Sixteen, father.

The priest passed his hand several times over his face. Then, resting his forehead against his hand, he leaned towards the grating and, with eyes still averted, spoke slowly. His voice was weary and old.

– You are very young, my child, he said, and let me implore of you to give up that sin. It is a terrible sin. It kills the body and it kills the soul. It is the cause of many crimes and misfortunes. Give it up, my child, for God's sake. It is dishonourable and unmanly. You cannot know where that wretched habit will lead you or where it will come against you. As long as you commit that sin, my poor child, you will never be worth one farthing to God. Pray to our mother Mary to help you. She will help you, my child. Pray to Our Blessed Lady when that sin comes into your mind. I am sure you will do that, will you not? You repent of all those sins. I am sure you do. And you will promise God now that by His holy grace you will never offend Him any more by that wicked sin. You will make that solemn promise to God, will you not?

– Yes, father.

The old and weary voice fell like sweet rain upon his quaking parching heart. How sweet and sad!

– Do so, my poor child. The devil has led you astray. Drive him back to hell when he tempts you to dishonour your body in that way – the foul spirit who hates Our Lord. Promise God now that you will give up that sin, that wretched wretched sin.

Blinded by his tears and by the light of God's mercifulness he bent his head and heard the grave words of absolution spoken and saw the priest's hand raised above him in token of forgiveness.

– God bless you, my child. Pray for me.

He knelt to say his penance, praying in a corner of the dark nave: and his prayers ascended to heaven from his purified heart like perfume streaming upwards from a heart of white rose.

The muddy streets were gay. He strode homeward, conscious of an invisible grace pervading and making light his limbs. In spite of all he had done it. He had confessed and God had pardoned him. His soul was made fair and holy once more, holy and happy.

It would be beautiful to die if God so willed. It was beautiful to live if God so willed, to live in grace a life of peace and virtue and forbearance with others.

James Joyce (1882–1941), *A Portrait of the Artist as a Young Man*, chapter 3.

A bar of good soap

Some of the features of the traditional rite, to which exception was taken, emerge with particular force in this sustained critique from Carol Ann Duffy. Between the traditional words the penitent's soul is worked like a puppet's as it timidly lists its sins according to convention, and is urged to fear damnation. One ambiguous element is the reference to the vinegar and sponge which were offered by his tormentors as a form of relief to Christ on the Cross (Mark 15:36). On the lips of the priest it is probably intended as a reminder of the sufferings of Christ by which the grace of forgiveness has been secured for us. But the reference may perhaps also be read subversively, against the speaker's intention, to suggest a guilty God offering relief to penitents who are more innocent than they realize.

Come away into this dark cell and tell
your sins to a hidden man your guardian angel
works your conscience like a glove-puppet It
smells in here doesn't it does it smell
like a coffin how would you know C'mon
out with them sins those little maggoty things
that wriggle in the soul... *Bless me Father*...

Just how bad have you been there's no water
in hell merely to think of a wrong's as evil
as doing it... *For I have sinned*... Penance
will cleanse you like a bar of good soap so
say the words into the musty gloom aye

on your knees let's hear that wee voice
recite transgression in the manner approved... *Forgive me...*

You do well to stammer A proper respect
for eternal damnation see the flicker
of your white hands clasping each other like
Hansel and Gretel in the big black wood
cross yourself Remember the vinegar and sponge
there's light on the other side of the door... *Mother
of God...* if you can only reach it Jesus loves you.

Carol Ann Duffy, 'Confession' from Mean Time (1993).

A chance to salvage everything

Here, as with Joyce, we have a much more positive presentation of the possibilities and hope which confession can bring about. A confessor speaks of the divine promise that all can be 'salvaged' and 'replenished', and assigns as a formal penance the translation of a poem by the sixteenth-century Spanish mystic St John of the Cross (Juan de la Cruz). That translation of 'Cantar del alma ... ' ('Song of the Soul ... ') forms the second half of the poem. The translation becomes what the confessor advises, a poem read as a prayer, in which the saint's image of a dark night of the soul is transformed by the trinitarian God, who is at once the 'source', 'fountain' and 'current' which gives refreshment and life.

As if the prisms of the kaleidoscope
I plunged once in a butt of muddied water
surfaced like a marvellous lightship

and out of its silted crystals a monk's face
that had spoken years ago from behind a grille
spoke again about the need and chance

to salvage everything, to re-envisage
the zenith and glimpsed jewels of any gift
mistakenly abased ...

What came to nothing could always be replenished.
'Read poems as prayers,' he said, 'and for your penance
translate me something by Juan de la Cruz.'

Returned from Spain to our chapped wilderness,
his consonants aspirate, his forehead shining,
he had made me feel there was nothing to confess.

Now his sandalled passage stirred me on to this:
How well I know that fountain, filling, running,
       although it is the night.

That eternal fountain, hidden away,
I know its haven and its secrecy
       although it is the night.

But not its source because it does not have one,
which is all sources' source and origin
       although it is the night.

No other thing can be so beautiful.
Here the earth and heaven drink their fill
       although it is the night.

So pellucid it never can be muddied,
and I know that all light radiates from it
       although it is the night.

I know no sounding-line can find its bottom,
nobody ford or plumb its deepest fathom
       although it is the night.

And its current so in flood it overspills
to water hell and heaven and all peoples
       although it is the night.

And the current that is generated there,
as far as it wills to, it can flow that far
       although it is the night.

And from these two a third current proceeds
which neither of these two, I know, precedes
       although it is the night.

This eternal fountain hides and splashes
within this living bread that is life to us
       although it is the night.

Hear it calling out to every creature.
And they drink these waters, although it is dark here
       because it is the night.

I am repining for this living fountain.
Within this bread of life I see it plain
       although it is the night.

                    Seamus Heaney (b. 1939), from *Station Island*.

Tell all

Though stress upon the indispensability of regular confession before a priest was not to reach its culmination till the Counter-Reformation period, already under Pope Innocent III, at the Fourth Lateran Council in 1215, an annual confession and communion had been enjoined upon all Western Christians. The pattern which then came to be followed was confession on Shrove Tuesday, followed by acts of penance during the 'forty days' of Lent, culminating in the actual taking of communion at Easter or 'Pasch' (a name deriving from its coincidence with the Jewish Passover). It is this pattern which is reflected in Dunbar's poem. Possibly a Franciscan novice, he was part of the flowering of Scottish culture which took place under James IV. The poem urges proper care in the recollection of sins, for only after a full confession will the penitent be properly 'shriven', 'assigned a proper penance', and thus be wholly absolved.

O sinful man, these are the forty dayis	*(of Lent)*
That every man sulde wilful penance dre;	*endure*
Our Lord Jesu, as haly writ sayis,	
Fastit himself our exampil to be;	
Sen sic ane michty king and lord as he	*since such*
To fast and pray was so obedient,	
We sinful folk sulde be more diligent.	
I reid thee, man, of thy transgressioun,	*advise/for*
With all thy heart that thou be penitent;	
Thou schrive thee clean and make confessioun,	
And see thereto that thou be diligent,	*also*
With all thy sins into thy mind present,	
That every sin by thyself be schawin,	*shown*
To thine confessour it ma be kend and knawin.	*known*
Upon thy body if thou hast ane wound	
That causes thee great painis for to feel,	
There is no leech ma mak thee hale and sound,	*doctor*
Till it be seen and clengit every deal;	*cleansed/part*
Richt so thy shrift, but it be schawin well:	
Thou art nocht able remissioun for to get,	
Wittandly and thou ane sin forget.	*knowingly if*
Of twenty woundis and ane be left unhelit	*unhealed*
What availis the leeching of the laif?	*remainder*
Richt so thy shrift, and there be oucht concelit,	*anything*
It availis nocht thy sely soul to saif;	*poor/save*
Nor yet of God remissioun for to haif:	
Of sin if thou wald have deliverance,	
Thou sulde it tell with all the circumstance.	

See that thy confessour be wise and discreit,
   That can thee discharge of every doubt and weir,   *uncertainty*
And power has of thy sinës compleit:
   If thow can nocht show forth thy sins perqueir,   *by heart*
   And he be blind, and can nocht at thee speir,   *ask*
Thou ma richt well in thy mind consider
That ane blind man is led forth by another.

And so I hald that ye are baith beguiled;
   He can nocht speir, nor thou can nocht him tell,
When, nor how, thy conscience thou has filed;   *defiled*
   Therefore, I reid, that thou excuse thysel,   *exonerate*
   And rype thy mind how every thing befell,   *search*
The time, the place, and how, and in what wyis,   *manner*
So that thy confessioun ma thy sins price.   *equal in value*

Avise thee well, ere thou come to the priest,   *bethink*
   Of all thy sins and namely of the maist,   *particularly*
That they be ready prentit in thy breast;   *printed*
   Thou sulde nocht come to shrive thee in haste,
   And syne sit doun abasit as ane beast: *afterwards*
With humble heart and sad contritioun,
Thou suld come to thine confessioun.

With thine awin mouth thy sinës thou suld tell;   *own*
   But sit and hear the priest has nocht ado.   *except to*
Wha kens thy sinës better na thysel?   *than*
   Therefore, I reid thee, take good tent thereto;   *heed*
   Thou knawis best where bindis thee thy shoe;   *pinches*
Therefore, be wise afore ere thou there come,
That thou schaw forth thy sinës all and some.

Where seldin compt is tane,   *account*
     and has a heavy charge,   *and [a person] has*
   And syne is reckless in his governance,   *afterwards*
And on his conscience he takes all too large,
   And on the end has no rememberance,
   That man is able to fall ane great mischance.
The sinful man that all the year o'er settis   *sets aside*
Fra Pasche to Pasche, richt many a thing forgettis.   *Easter/forgets*

I reid thee, man, while thou art stark and young,   *strong*
   With pith and strength unto thy yearis green,
While thou art able baith in mind and tongue,
   Repent thee, man, and keep thy conscience clean.
   Till bide till age is many peril seen: *to wait until old age*

Small merit is of sinës for to irk   *tire*
When thou art old and ma na wrangis work.   *wrongs/do*

William Dunbar (*c.* 1460–*c.* 1515), 'The Manner of Passing to Confession'.

The lawless leg

Some of Burns's most famous lines come in the poem 'To a Louse': 'O wad
some Pow'r the giftie gie us / To see oursels as others see us!' Burns had
personally witnessed the public humiliation of the 'repenting stool' that was
enforced under the Presbyterianism of his day. In this poem he turns his
satire on an elder within that system, who clearly has no consciousness of
his own guilt. Amidst all the humour the poem is a warning about the need
for self-examination – attempting to see ourselves as others see us. The
sacramentalist would, of course, argue that such insight is most likely to
come through the mediation and counsel of others.

> O Thou that in the Heavens does dwell,
> Wha, as it pleases best Thysel,
> Sends ane to Heaven an' ten to Hell
>   A' for Thy glory,
> And no for onie guid or ill
>   They've done before Thee!
>
> I bless and praise Thy matchless might,
> When thousands Thou hast left in night,
> That I am here before Thy sight,
>   For gifts an' grace
> A burning and a shining light
>   To a' this place. . . .
>
> But yet, O Lord! confess I must:
> At times I'm fash'd wi' fleshly lust;   *irked*
> An' sometimes, too, in warldly trust,
>   Vile self gets in;
> But Thou remembers we are dust,
>   Defiled wi' sin.
>
> O Lord! yestreen, Thou kens, wi' Meg –   *last night/knowest*
> Thy pardon I sincerely beg –
> O, may't ne'er be a living plague
>   To my dishonour!
> An' I'll ne'er lift a lawless leg
>   Again upon her. . . .
>
> Maybe Thou lets this fleshly thorn
> Buffet Thy servant e'en and morn,

Lest he owre proud and high should turn
    That he's sae gifted:
If sae, Thy han' maun e'en be borne   *must*
    Until Thou lift it.

Lord, bless Thy chosen in this place,
For here Thou has a chosen race!
But God confound their stubborn face
    An' blast their name,
Wha bring Thy elders to disgrace
    An' open shame! ...

Lord, hear my earnest cry and pray'r
Against that Presbyt'ry of Ayr!
Thy strong right hand, Lord, mak it bare
    Upo' their heads!
Lord, visit them, an' dinna spare,   *do not*
    For their misdeeds! ...

But, Lord, remember me and mine
Wi' mercies temporal and divine,
That I for grace an' gear may shine   *wealth*
    Excell'd by nane;
And a' the glory shall be Thine –
    Amen, Amen!

Robert Burns (1759–96), from 'Holy Willie's
Prayer'.

Ice not fire

Self-perception, however, sometimes comes despite, and not because of, our efforts. In her short story 'The Enduring Chill' Flannery O'Connor describes the sacrament working its effect almost despite the intentions of both priest and 'penitent'. Asbury has caught a fever from drinking unpasteurized milk while showing off to his mother's farm-hands. Bored by confinement, and using the alleged seriousness of his condition as a pretext, he asks for a priest to be summoned, preferably a Jesuit, so that he can 'discuss something besides the weather'. The attempt at intellectual conversation is a complete disaster. Nonetheless not long after this the cold chill of the reality that Asbury had hitherto avoided facing finally descends. Despite his intellectual incompetence the priest has induced a changed perspective, a not altogether welcome conversion.

'Who made you?' the priest asked in a martial tone.

'Different people believe different things about that,' Asbury said.

'God made you,' the priest said shortly. 'Who is God?'

'God is an idea created by man,' Asbury said, feeling that he was getting into stride, that two could play at this.

'God is a spirit infinitely perfect,' the priest said. 'You are a very ignorant boy. Why did God make you?'

'God didn't ...'

'God made you to know Him, to love Him, to serve Him in this world and to be happy with Him in the next!' the old priest said in a battering voice. 'If you don't apply yourself to the catechism how do you expect to know how to save your immortal soul?'

Asbury saw he had made a mistake and that it was time to get rid of the old fool. 'Listen,' he said, 'I'm not a Roman.'

'A poor excuse for not saying your prayers!' the old man snorted.

Asbury slumped slightly in the bed. 'I'm dying,' he shouted.

'But you're not dead yet!' said the priest, 'and how do you expect to meet God face to face when you've never spoken to Him? How do you expect to get what you don't ask for? God does not send the Holy Ghost to those who don't ask for Him. Ask Him to send the Holy Ghost.'

'The Holy Ghost?' Asbury said.

'Are you so ignorant you've never heard of the Holy Ghost?' the priest asked.

'Certainly I've heard of the Holy Ghost' Asbury said furiously, 'and the Holy Ghost is the last thing I'm looking for!'

'And He may be the last thing you get,' the priest said, his one fierce eye inflamed. 'Do you want your soul to suffer eternal damnation? Do you want to be deprived of God for all eternity? Do you want to suffer the most terrible pain, greater than fire, the pain of loss? Do you want to suffer the pain of loss for all eternity?'

Asbury moved his arms and legs helplessly as if he were pinned to the bed by the terrible eye.

'How can the Holy Ghost fill your soul when it's full of trash?' the priest roared. 'The Holy Ghost will not come until you see yourself as you are – a lazy ignorant conceited youth!' he said, pounding his fist on the little bedside table.

Mrs. Fox burst in. 'Enough of this!' she cried. 'How dare you talk that way to a poor sick boy? You're upsetting him. You'll have to go.'

'The poor lad doesn't even know his catechism,' the priest said, rising. 'I should think you would have taught him to say his daily prayers. You have neglected your duty as his mother.' He turned back to the bed and said affably, 'I'll give you my blessing and after this you must say your daily prayers without fail,' whereupon he put his hand on Asbury's head and rumbled something in Latin. 'Call me any time,' he said, 'and we can have another little chat,' and then he followed Mrs. Fox's rigid back out. The last thing Asbury heard him say was, 'He's a good lad at heart but very ignorant.' ...

Asbury sat up again. He turned his head, almost surreptitiously, to the side where the key he had given his mother was lying on the bedside table. His hand shot out and closed over it and returned it to his pocket. He glanced across the room into the small oval-framed dresser mirror. The eyes that stared back at him were the same that had returned his gaze every day from that mirror but it seemed to him that they were paler. They looked shocked clean as if they had been prepared for some awful vision about to come down on him. He shuddered and turned his head quickly the other way and stared out the window. A blinding red-gold sun moved serenely from under a purple cloud. Below it the treeline was black against the crimson sky. It formed a brittle wall, standing as if it were the frail defense he had set up in his mind to protect him from what was coming. The boy fell back on his pillow and stared at the ceiling. His limbs that had been racked for so many weeks by fever and chill were numb now. The old life in him was exhausted. He awaited the coming of new. It was then that he felt the beginning of a chill, a chill so peculiar, so light, that it was like a warm ripple across a deeper sea of cold. His breath came short. The fierce bird which through the years of his childhood and the days of his illness had been poised over his head, waiting mysteriously, appeared all at once to be in motion. Asbury blanched and the last film of illusion was torn as if by a whirlwind from his eyes. He saw that for the rest of his days, frail, racked, but enduring, he would live in the face of a purifying terror. A feeble cry, a last impossible protest escaped him. But the Holy Ghost, emblazoned in ice instead of fire, continued, implacable, to descend.

Flannery O'Connor (1925–64), 'The Enduring Chill' from *Everything That Rises Must Converge.*

A New England heretic

In Flannery O'Connor's story confession 'worked', despite the absence of any expectations on Asbury's part. However, the problem is sometimes that expectations are too restricted. In his final novel, *The Marble Faun*, the Massachusetts novelist Nathaniel Hawthorne reflects on a two-year sojourn in Italy. Hilda has witnessed a murder and, though of Puritan background, finds herself seeking release in a Vatican confessional. Underlying the whole passage is an irony which implies a view transcending the theologies of both penitent and priest: though Hilda denies that any can give absolution except God she finds her worries dissolved by her confession; though the priest offers both solace and reassurance, he insists that the sacrament is effective only within the confines of his own church.

> When Hilda had almost completed the circuit of the transept, she came to a confessional, (the central part was closed, but a mystic rod protruded from it, indicating the presence of a priest within,) on which was inscribed, PRO ANGLICA LINGUA.
>
> It was the word in season! If she had heard her mother's voice from within the tabernacle, calling her, in her own mother-tongue, to come and lay her poor head in her lap, and sob out all her troubles, Hilda could not have responded with a more inevitable obedience. She did not think; she only felt. Within her heart, was a great need. Close at hand, within the veil of the confessional, was the relief. She flung herself down in the penitent's place; and, tremulously, passionately, with sobs, tears, and the turbulent overflow of emotion too long repressed, she poured out the dark story which had infused its poison into her innocent life. . . .
>
> After she had ceased to speak, Hilda heard the priest bestir himself with an old man's reluctant movement. He stept out of the confessional; and as the girl was still kneeling in the penitential corner, he summoned her forth.
>
> 'Stand up, my daughter!' said the mild voice of the Confessor. 'What we have further to say, must be spoken face to face.'
>
> Hilda did his bidding, and stood before him with a downcast visage, which flushed, and grew pale again. But it had the wonderful beauty which we may often observe in those who have recently gone through a great struggle, and won the peace that lies just on the other side. We see it in a new mother's face; we see it in the faces of the dead; and in Hilda's countenance, (which had always a rare natural charm for her friends,) this glory of peace made her as lovely as an angel. . . .

'It has not escaped my observation, daughter,' said the priest, 'that this is your first acquaintance with the confessional. How is this?'

'Father,' replied Hilda raising her eyes, and again letting them fall, 'I am of New England birth, and was bred as what you call a heretic.'

'From New England?' exclaimed the priest. 'It was my own birth-place, likewise; nor have fifty years of absence made me cease to love it. But, a heretic! And are you reconciled to the Church?'

'Never, Father,' said Hilda.

'And, that being the case,' demanded the old man, 'on what ground, my daughter, have you sought to avail yourself of these blessed privileges (confined exclusively to members of the one true Church) of Confession and Absolution?'

'Absolution, Father?' exclaimed Hilda, shrinking back. 'Oh, no, no! I never dreamed of that! Only our Heavenly Father can forgive my sins; and it is only by sincere repentance of whatever wrong I may have done, and by my own best efforts towards a higher life, that I can hope for His forgiveness! God forbid that I should ask absolution from mortal man!'

'Then, wherefore,' rejoined the priest, with somewhat less mildness in his tone – 'wherefore, I ask again, have you taken possession, as I may term it, of this holy ordinance; being a heretic, and neither seeking to share, nor having faith in, the unspeakable advantages which the Church offers to its penitents?'

'Father,' answered Hilda, trying to tell the old man the simple truth, 'I am a motherless girl, and a stranger here in Italy. I had only God to take care of me, and be my closest friend; and the terrible, terrible crime, which I have revealed to you, thrust itself between Him and me; so that I groped for Him in the darkness, as it were, and found Him not – found nothing but a dreadful solitude, and this crime in the midst of it! I could not bear it. It seemed as if I made the awful guilt my own, by keeping it hidden in my heart. I grew a fearful thing to myself. I was going mad!'

'It was a grievous trial, my poor child!' observed the Confessor. 'Your relief, I trust, will prove to be greater than you yet know.'

'I feel already how immense it is!' said Hilda, looking gratefully in his face. 'Surely, Father, it was the hand of Providence that led me hither, and made me feel that this vast temple of Christianity, this great home of Religion, must needs contain

some cure, some ease, at least, for my unutterable anguish. And
it has proved so. I have told the hideous secret; told it under the
sacred seal of the Confessional; and now it will burthen my poor
heart no more!'

Nathaniel Hawthorne (1806–64), The Marble Faun, chapter 39.

The doctor's remedy

Like Hawthorne, Edmund Spenser is concerned to enlarge our sense of the
various ways in which the divine forgiveness can be sacramentally mediated
through others. In this extract from his greatest poem, *The Faerie Queene*,
the Redcross knight, St George, symbolizing the Christian Everyman,
having fallen prey to despair at his own sinfulness, is brought to the House
of Holiness by 'Una', who represents truth and the one true church (which,
for Spenser, means Anglicanism). There 'Caelia' (heavenly grace) intro-
duces the knight to the theological virtues, Faith ('Fidelia') and Hope
('Speranza'). Fortified by them, he passes through the traditional stages of
confession, absolution, penance, and resolution not to sin again. Spenser
would have been familiar with what is now the First Exhortation in the 1662
Prayer Book Holy Communion service, which legitimates private confession
to a priest – though there is nothing to indicate that the confessor here,
'Patience', is a priest. None the less, the general tone is thoroughly
sacramental, given its repeated refrain that it is only through the mediation
of the Church as a whole that the divine forgiveness can be appropriated.

> The faithful knight now grew in little space,
>   By hearing her [Caelia], and by her sister's lore,
>   To such perfection of all heavenly grace,
>   That wretched world he 'gan for to abhor,
>   And mortal life 'gan loathe, as thing forlore,   *lost*
>   Grieved with remembrance of his wicked ways,
>   And pricked with anguish of his sins so sore,
>   That he desired to end his wretched days:
> So much the dart of sinful guilt the soul dismays.
>
> But wise *Speranza* gave him comfort sweet,   *Hope*
>   And taught him how to take assurèd hold
>   Upon her silver anchor, as was meet;
>   Else had his sins so great and manifold
>   Made him forget all that *Fidelia* told.
>   In this distressèd doubtful agony,   *fearful*
>   When him his dearest *Una* did behold,
>   Disdaining life, desiring leave to die,
> She found herself assailed with great perplexity.

And came to *Caelia* to declare her smart,
   Who well acquainted with that common plight,
   Which sinful horror works in wounded heart,   *horror of sin*
   Her wisely comforted all that she might,
   With goodly counsel and advisement right;   *advice*
   And straightway sent with careful diligence,
   To fetch a leech, the which had great insight   *doctor*
   In that disease of grievèd conscience,
And well could cure the same: his name was *Patience*.

Who coming to that soul-diseasèd knight,
   Could hardly him entreat to tell his grief;
   Which known, and all that noyed   *troubled*
      his heavy spright   *spirit*
   Well searched, eftsoons he 'gan apply relief   *probed/presently*
   Of salves and med'cines, which had
      passing prief,   *great efficacy*
   And thereto added words of wondrous might,   *(absolution)*
   By which to ease he him recurèd brief,   *restored/quickly*
   And much assuaged the passion of his plight,   *suffering*
That he his pain endured, as seeming now more light.

But yet the cause and root of all his ill,
   Inward corruption, and infected sin,
   Not purged nor healed, behind remainèd still,
   And festering sore did rankle yet within,
   Close creeping 'twixt the marrow and the skin.
   Which to extirp, he laid him privily   *root out*
   Down in a darksome lowly place far in,
   Whereas he meant his corsives to apply,   *caustic remedies*
And with strait diet tame his stubborn malady.   *strict*

In ashes and sackcloth he did array
   His dainty corse, proud humours to abate,   *handsome body*
   And dieted with fasting every day,
   The swelling of his wounds to mitigate,
   And made him pray both early and eke late: *also*
   And ever as superfluous flesh did rot
   Amendment ready still at hand did wait,
   To pluck it out with pincers fiery hot,
That soon in him was left no one corrupted jot.

And bitter *Penance* with an iron whip,
   Was wont him once to disple every day;   *discipline*
   And sharp *Remorse* his heart did prick and nip,

That drops of blood thence like a well did play;
And sad *Repentance* usèd to embay   *drench*
His body in salt water smarting sore,
The filthy blots of sin to wash away.
So in short space they did to health restore
The man that would not live, but erst lay at death's door. *once*

In which his torment often was so great
That like a lion he would cry and roar,
And rend his flesh, and his own sinews eat.
His own dear *Una* hearing evermore
His rueful shrieks and groanings often tore
Her guiltless garments, and her golden hair,
For pity of his pain and anguish sore;
Yet all with patience wisely she did bear,
For well she wist his crime could else be never clear.   *knew*

Edmund Spenser (*c.* 1552–99), from *The Faerie Queene*,
Book I, Canto X.

Forget and forgive

Portia's famous praise of mercy in *The Merchant of Venice* (IV. i) culminates
in the declaration: 'It is an attribute to God himself, / And earthly power
doth then show likest God's / When mercy seasons justice'. In *King Lear* –
which, despite its pagan setting, can be seen as Christian in ethos – that
insight is carried a stage further, in Cordelia's willingness to forgive her
father's unjust rejection of her, and in his contrition. Cordelia's echo of
Christ's words, 'O dear father / It is thy business that I go about' (IV. iv;
Luke 2:49), may even be taken to imply that a Christian reading was
intended. Whether or not this is so, the play well illustrates the wider sense
in which divine forgiveness can be mediated sacramentally through the
actions of others.

    Cordelia.   O my dear father, restoration hang
Thy medicine on my lips, and let this kiss
Repair those violent harms that my two sisters
Have in thy reverence made!
    Kent.   Kind and dear princess!
    Cordelia.   Had you not been their father, these white flakes
Did challenge pity of them. Was this a face
To be opposed against the warring winds?
To stand against the deep dread-bolted thunder
In the most terrible and nimble stroke
Of quick cross lightning? To watch – poor perdu! –
With this thin helm? Mine enemy's dog,
Though he had bit me, should have stood that night

Against my fire; and wast thou fain, poor father,
To hovel thee with swine and rogues forlorn,
In short and musty straw? Alack, alack!
'Tis wonder that thy life and wits at once
Had not concluded all. He wakes; speak to him.
 Doctor. Madam, do you; 'tis fittest.
 Cordelia. How does my royal lord? How fares your
  Majesty?
 Lear. You do me wrong to take me out o'th'grave:
Thou art a soul in bliss; but I am bound
Upon a wheel of fire, that mine own tears
Do scald like molten lead.
 Cordelia. Sir, do you know me?
 Lear. You are a spirit, I know; when did you die?
 Cordelia. Still, still, far wide!
 Doctor. He's scarce awake; let him alone awhile.
 Lear. Where have I been? Where am I? Fair daylight?
I am mightily abused; I should e'en die with pity
To see another thus. I know not what to say.
I will not swear these are my hands: let's see;
I feel this pin prick. Would I were assured
Of my condition!
 Cordelia. [*Kneels*] O, look upon me, sir,
And hold your hand in benediction o'er me;
No, sir, you must not kneel.
 Lear. Pray do not mock me;
I am a very foolish fond old man,
Fourscore and upward, not an hour more nor less;
And, to deal plainly,
I fear I am not in my perfect mind.
Methinks I should know you, and know this man,
Yet I am doubtful: for I am mainly ignorant
What place this is; and all the skill I have
Remembers not these garments, nor I know not
Where I did lodge last night. Do not laugh at me,
For (as I am a man) I think this lady
To be my child Cordelia.
 Cordelia. And so I am: I am!
 Lear. Be your tears wet? Yes, faith: I pray weep not.
If you have poison for me, I will drink it:
I know you do not love me, for your sisters
Have (as I do remember) done me wrong;
You have some cause; they have not.

Cordelia.   No cause, no cause. . . .
   Lear. You must bear with me. Pray you now, forget
and forgive; I am old and foolish.

William Shakespeare (1564–1616), *King Lear*, from Act IV, scene vii.

Gluttony's vomit

Though Hawthorne and Spenser were both Protestants, one should not
assume that their wider notion of sacramental mediation is not also found in
Catholic writers. Much of Langland's *Piers Plowman* is concerned with
attacking the corruptions of the medieval clergy, and for this reason
Langland is sometimes seen as having sympathized with his contemporary,
Wyclif, and the Lollards, and so as having anticipated the Reformation.
Whether so or not, certainly in this case it is the rebukes of the Glutton's
wife which provide the spur to repentance, while the subsequent confession
makes no mention of the presence of a priest. Though Langland's portrayal
of the Seven Deadly Sins offers a lively and amusing depiction of medieval
life and its excesses, he ends on a more serious, though hopeful note.
Quoting the words of the Easter liturgy, he observes that it was a 'happy
fault' which allowed the possibility of human sin, because it is this which
made the incarnation necessary, and so made possible our own identification with Christ.

There was laughing and louring and	*scowling*
'let go the cup!'	*pass round the cup*
Bargains and beverages began to rise,	
And seten so till evensong, and sung some while,	*they sat*
Till Glutton had yglubbed a gallon and a gill.	*gulped down*
He pissed a potel, in a	*half a gallon*
pater noster while,	*time it takes to say an 'Our Father'*
And blew his round ruwet	*trumpet*
at the ruggebone's end,	*backbone's*
That all that hearden that horn held their nose after,	
And wished it had been wexed with a wisp of furse.	*wax-polished*
He might neither step nor stand, ere he his staff had,	
And then 'gan he to go like a gleman's bitch,	*walk/minstrel's*
Some time aside, and some time arere,	*backwards*
As whoso layeth lines for to latch fowls.	*catch birds*
And when he drough to the door,	*drew*
then dimmed his eyen.	*grew dim*
He thrumbled on the threshold and	*jostled*
threw to the earth.	*fell*
Clement the cobbler caught him by the middle	*waist*

For to lift him aloft, and laid him on his knees.
Ac Glutton was a great churl and a grim in the lifting,   *but*
And coughed up a cawdel in Clement's lap.   *mess*
Is none so hungry hound in Hertfordshire
Durst lap of that leaving, so unlovely it smaught!   *smelled*
With all the woe of this world, his wife and his wenche   *servant*
Bear him to his bed, and brought him therein.
And after all this excess he had an accidie,   *attack of sloth*
That he slept Saturday and Sunday, till sun yede to rest.   *went*
Then waked he of his wynking, and wiped his eyen;   *sleep*
The first word that he spake was, 'Where is the bowl?'
His wife edwyted him then how wickedly he lived,   *reproached*
And Repentance right so rebuked him that time:
'As thou with words and works hast wrought evil in thy life,
Shrive thee and be shamed thereof,   *confess*
          and show it with thy mouth.'   *reveal*
'I, Glutton,' quoth the gome, 'guilty me yield,   *man*
That I have trespassed with my tongue, I can not tell how oft
Sworn "God's soul and his sides!" and
          "So help me God and halidome!"   *relics*
There no need was nine hundred times;
And overseyen me at supper   *forgotten myself*
          and some time at nones,   *(afternoon prayer)*
That I, Glutton, girte it up ere I had gone a mile,   *vomited*
And yspilt that might be spared   *wasted/saved*
          and spended on some hungry;   *hungry person*
Over-delicately on feasting days drunken and eaten both,
And sat sometimes so long there that I slept and ate at once.
For love of tales in taverns into drink the more I dived;
And hied to the meat ere noon on fasting days.'   *hastened/food*
'This showing shrift,' quoth Repentance,
          'shall be merit to thee.' ...   *open confession*
And then had Repentance ruth and red them all to kneel.   *instructed*
'For I shall beseech for all sinful our Saviour of grace
To amenden us of our misdeeds and do mercy to us all.   *have ... on*
Now God,' quoth he, 'that of Thy goodness
          gonne the world make,   *made the world*
And of naught madest aught, and man most like to thyself,   *all*
And sithen suffredst him to sin,   *afterwards permitted*
          a sickness to us all –
And all for the best, as I believe,
          whatever the Book telleth,   *(the Bible)*

O felix culpa! O necessarium peccatum Ade!
[O happy fault! O necessary sin of Adam!]
For through that sin Thy Son sent was to this earth
And became man of a maid mankind to save;
And madest Thyself with Thy Son   *through*
    us sinful ylike.' ...   *like us sinful people*
'And by so much it seemeth the sikerer we mowe   *more surely/can*
Bid and beseech, if it be Thy will,   *pray*
That art our Father and our Brother, be merciable to us, *merciful*
And have ruth on these ribaudes   *mercy/sinners*
    that repenten them sore   *earnestly*
That ever they wrathed Thee in this world,   *angered*
    in word, thought or deed!'

William Langland (c. 1330–c. 1386), from Piers Plowman, Passus V.

Nature's curse and release

Sometimes it is neither priest nor Church as a whole, nor specific individuals who play the key role, but God's non-human creation. In *The Rime
of the Ancient Mariner* the ship on which the mariner is sailing looks likely
to founder on ice, when an albatross appears as a bird of good omen and all
is well. But inexplicably the mariner shoots it, and fresh disaster befalls.
The boat is becalmed, and, to indicate whom they blame, the mariner's
shipmates hang the dead bird round his neck. Worse is to follow in the death
of the crew. (The following extract begins at this point.) The story ends with
the mariner formally 'shriven' by a holy hermit, but the sacramental
mediation begins earlier, with God's creation itself healing him. For it is his
love of the beauty of the water-snakes ('God's creatures of the great calm' as
Coleridge describes them in a marginal gloss) that causes the albatross to
fall from his neck. The poem ends, as it began, with the mariner explaining
his periodic compulsion to tell his story. Unlike those who testify to the
liberating and purifying effects of confession, the mariner has, it seems, a
neurotic guilt which confession only temporarily alleviates.

    I looked upon the rotting sea,
    And drew my eyes away;
    I looked upon the rotting deck,
    And there the dead men lay.

    I looked to heaven, and tried to pray;
    But or ever a prayer had gusht,
    A wicked whisper came, and made
    My heart as dry as dust.

    I closed my lids, and kept them close,
    And the balls like pulses beat;

For the sky and the sea, and the sea and the sky
Lay like a load on my weary eye,
And the dead were at my feet.

The cold sweat melted from their limbs,
Nor rot nor reek did they:
The look with which they looked on me
Had never passed away.

An orphan's curse would drag to hell
A spirit from on high;
But oh! more horrible than that
Is the curse in a dead man's eye!
Seven days, seven nights, I saw that curse,
And yet I could not die.

The moving Moon went up the sky,
And no where did abide:
Softly she was going up,
And a star or two beside –

Her beams bemocked the sultry main,
Like April hoar-frost spread;
But where the ship's huge shadow lay,
The charmèd water burnt alway
A still and awful red.

Beyond the shadow of the ship,
I watched the water-snakes:
They moved in tracks of shining white,
And when they reared, the elfish light
Fell off in hoary flakes.

Within the shadow of the ship
I watched their rich attire:
Blue, glossy green, and velvet black,
They coiled and swam; and every track
Was a flash of golden fire.

O happy living things! no tongue
Their beauty might declare:
A spring of love gushed from my heart,
And I blessed them unaware:
Sure my kind saint took pity on me,
And I blessed them unaware.

The self-same moment I could pray;
And from my neck so free

The Albatross fell off, and sank
Like lead into the sea. . . .

But soon I heard the dash of oars,
I heard the Pilot's cheer;
My head was turned perforce away
And I saw a boat appear.

The Pilot and the Pilot's boy,
I heard them coming fast:
Dear Lord in Heaven! it was a joy
The dead men could not blast.

I saw a third – I heard his voice:
It is the Hermit good!
He singeth loud his godly hymns
That he makes in the wood.
He'll shrieve my soul, he'll wash away
The Albatross's blood. . . .

'O shrieve me, shrieve me, holy man!'
The Hermit crossed his brow.
'Say quick,' quoth he, 'I bid thee say –
What manner of man art thou?'

Forthwith this frame of mine was wrenched
With a woful agony,
Which forced me to begin my tale;
And then it left me free.

Since then, at an uncertain hour,
That agony returns:
And till my ghastly tale is told,
This heart within me burns.

I pass, like night, from land to land;
I have strange power of speech;
That moment that his face I see,
I know the man that must hear me:
To him my tale I teach. . . .

He prayeth well, who loveth well
Both man and bird and beast.

He prayeth best, who loveth best
All things both great and small;
For the dear God who loveth us,
He made and loveth all.

Samuel Taylor Coleridge (1772–1834), from *The Rime of the Ancient Mariner*.

DEATH INTO LIFE

Introduction

The attempt to think of death in sacramental terms may sound initially self-contradictory, since by definition a sacrament requires the physical as its medium, whereas death involves destruction of the physical. But the conflict is only superficial. The first group of extracts illustrates this by reference to what in past centuries would have been called 'a good death'. For a Christian, the manner of death is in large part affected by whether or not the divine love is mediated at life's close. Hopkins' sonnet exhibits a priest's concern for a weakened and deranged parishioner, while Greene and Malory describe two very different ways in which sexual love seeks the transformation of the beloved. But it is perhaps Tolstoy who most effectively identifies this aspect of death's sacramental dimension, with the person seen as 'a particle of love' returning to its source.

That larger understanding should not be lost as we turn to the more narrowly institutional concept, that of priestly anointing before death. For what such anointing symbolizes is the desire to return to God a healthy soul, one redeemed by the Christian gospel of love. That to achieve this the *body* is anointed may seem paradoxical, but this reflects the traditional Christian holistic understanding of the person. This idea is found both in the Gospels (e.g. Mark 6:13) and in the Epistle of James (5:14–16), where the practice of anointing with oil is urged at one and the same time for physical healing and forgiveness of sins. Such anointing or 'unction' of the sick has been widely revived in a number of denominations. In its classical form this focused on the five senses, represented by the eyes, ears, nose, lips, and hands and feet (cf. Flaubert, Dowson). Catholic practice gradually confined its use to unction 'in extremis' (at the point of death), the Western tradition often using the term for the whole rite of last confession, anointing and final reception of communion. Anglicans traditionally did not so limit its use, and never called it 'extreme unction'. Protestant susceptibilities have sometimes been offended by the implied claim that a last-minute 'conversion' may be enough for salvation. Taylor helps identify some of these worries, while the extracts from Waugh and Flaubert nicely contrast with one another. Despite the beauty of the form Flaubert's late penitent fails, while Waugh's is clearly sincere.

The final selection illustrates what is perhaps the most obvious sense in which death might be seen as sacramental, and to which the practice of extreme unction already alludes. The credal affirmation of 'the resurrection of the body' is intended to assert the transformation of the whole person, and not the survival of just the soul, and this is one reason why the Empty Tomb has been seen as so important: the body is transformed, not destroyed (1 Cor 15:35–56). It is a hope beautifully expressed by Herbert. When found reflected in nature's recurring transformations (Kilvert), it returns us to 'The Sacramental World' with which this book began, though we leave Mary Coleridge with the last word: might sacraments cease to be, once we see God face to face?

To hell for love

Can the mediation of another transform the character of one's death? That is a central theme in Graham Greene's *Brighton Rock*. Pinkie is a teenage aspiring gang-leader. Rose, a young waitress, observes one of his crimes, but falls in love with him. Pursued by Ida who is trying to collect evidence against him, Pinkie decides to eliminate Rose by persuading her that the only solution for both of them is a joint suicide, which he intends to fake. Rose is a committed Roman Catholic for whom suicide will mean eternal damnation. He is only nominally Catholic, but familiar enough with the mass to quote its Latin correctly, as also to toy with the idea of last-minute repentance: 'between the stirrup and the ground'. The tension which runs throughout the novel between official Church teaching and the power of love to transform the significance of death reaches its culmination in the concluding scene, with Pinkie now dead and Rose in the confessional, still wanting to be with him even if damned, and, with the encouragement of the priest, determined to pray for his ultimate salvation. Here we take up the story at the suicide pact.

> 'We'll go and have a drink,' he said, 'and then – you'll see. I got everything settled.' He said with hideous ease, 'It won't take a minute.' He put his arm round her waist and his face was close to hers: she could see him now, considering and considering; his skin smelt of petrol: everything smelt of petrol in the little leaking out-dated car. She said, 'Are you sure ... can't we wait ... one day?'
>
> 'What's the good? You saw her there tonight. She's hanging on. One day she'll get her evidence. What's the use?'
>
> 'Why not *then*?'
>
> 'It might be too late *then*.' He said disjointedly through the flapping hood, 'A knock and the next thing you know ... the cuffs ... too late ... ' He said with cunning, 'We wouldn't be together

then.' He put down his foot and the needle quivered up to thirty-five – the old car wouldn't do more than forty, but it gave an immense impression of reckless speed: the wind battered on the glass and tore through the rent. He began softly to intone – 'Dona nobis pacem.'

'He won't.'

'What do you mean?'

'Give us peace.'

He thought: there'll be time enough in the years ahead – sixty years – to repent of this. Go to a priest. Say: 'Father, I've committed murder twice. And there was a girl – she killed herself.' Even if death came suddenly, driving home tonight, the smash on the lamp-post – there was still 'between the stirrup and the ground'. The houses on one side ceased altogether, and the sea came back to them, beating at the undercliff drive, a darkness and deep sound. He wasn't really deceiving himself – he'd learnt the other day that when the time was short there were other things than contrition to think about. It didn't matter anyway . . . he wasn't made for peace, he couldn't believe in it. Heaven was a word: hell was something he could trust. A brain was only capable of what it could conceive, and it couldn't conceive what it had never experienced; his cells were formed of the cement school-playground, the dead fire and the dying man in the St Pancras waiting-room, his bed at Frank's and his parents' bed. An awful resentment stirred in him – why shouldn't he have had his chance like all the rest, seen his glimpse of heaven if it was only a crack between the Brighton walls . . . He turned as they went down to Rottingdean and took a long look at her as if she might be it – but the brain couldn't conceive – he saw a mouth which wanted the sexual embrace, the shape of breasts demanding a child. Oh, she was good all right, he supposed, but she wasn't good enough: he'd got her down.

Above Rottingdean the new villas began: pipe-dream archi-tecture: up on the downs the obscure skeleton of a nursing home, winged like an aeroplane. He said, 'They won't hear us in the country.' The lights petered out along the road to Peace-haven: the chalk of a new cutting flapped like white sheets in the headlight: cars came down on them blinding them. He said, 'The battery's low.'

She had the sense that he was a thousand miles away – his thoughts had gone on beyond the act she couldn't tell where. He was wise; he was foreseeing, she thought, things she couldn't conceive – eternal punishment, the flames . . . She felt terror, the idea of pain shook her, their purpose drove up in a flurry of rain against the old stained windscreen. This road led nowhere else. It was said to be the worst act of all, the act of despair, the sin without forgiveness; sitting there in the smell of petrol she tried to realize despair, the mortal sin, but she couldn't; it didn't feel like despair. He was going to damn himself, but she was going to show them that they couldn't damn him without damning her too. There was nothing he could do, she wouldn't do: she felt capable of sharing any murder. A light lit his face and left it; a frown, a thought, a child's face. She felt responsibility move in her breasts; she wouldn't let him go into that darkness alone.

Graham Greene (1904–92), *Brighton Rock*, Part 7, chapter 7.

Ransoming reason's disorder

In this sonnet Hopkins reflects on the close relationship that has been built up between himself as priest and the dying person, and on the contrast between the weakened dependent man he tended and the man's physical power in youth and middle age. Great strength has been replaced by physical weakness and a rambling mind. Initially too, cursing took the place of goodness, but priestly love and care effected a transformation which was begun by the taking of communion ('our sweet reprieve and ransom') and completed by anointing at death.

Felix Randal the farrier, O he is dead then? my duty all ended,
Who have watched his mould of man, big-boned and hardy-
        handsome
Pining, pining, till time when reason rambled in it and some
Fatal four disorders, fleshed there, all contended?

Sickness broke him. Impatient he cursed at first, but mended
Being anointed and all; though a heavenlier heart began some
Months earlier, since I had our sweet reprieve and ransom
Tendered to him. Ah well, God rest him all road ever he
        offended!

This seeing the sick endears them to us, us too it endears.
My tongue had taught thee comfort, touch had quenched thy
        tears,
Thy tears that touched my heart, child, Felix, poor Felix
        Randal;

How far from then forethought of, all thy more boisterous
        years,

When thou at the random grim forge, powerful amidst peers,
Didst fettle for the great grey drayhorse his bright and
    battering sandal!

Gerard Manley Hopkins (1844–89), 'Felix Randal'.

Redeemed by human love

Malory's *Le Morte D'Arthur* marks the culmination of the medieval expansion of the Arthurian legends. Written while the author was in prison, his version, unlike many others, makes Launcelot unsuccessful in his quest for the Grail, the cup which caught the blood of the crucified Christ and is used as a symbol for Christian perfection. His illicit love for Queen Guenever has been to blame, but, when he learns that she has become a nun, spurred on by her devotion and example he becomes a priest. In this extract he is 'houseled and enelid' (given communion and anointed), and in confirmation of his changed state his bishop confessor dreams of his reception into heaven, while his earthly body is carried to his castle, Joyous Gard.

Then Sir Launcelot never after ate but little meat, ne drank, till he was dead. For then he sickened more and more, and dried, and dwined away. For the Bishop nor none of his fellows might not make him to eat, and little he drank, that he was waxen by a cubit shorter than he was, that the people could not know him. For evermore, day and night, he prayed, but sometime he slumbered a broken sleep; ever he was lying grovelling on the tomb of King Arthur and Queen Guenever. And there was no comfort that the Bishop, nor Sir Bors, nor none of his fellows, could make him, it availed not. So within six weeks after, Sir Launcelot fell sick, and lay in his bed; and then he sent for the Bishop that there was hermit, and all his true fellows. Then Sir Launcelot said with dreary steven: Sir Bishop, I pray you give to me all my rites that longeth to a Christian man. It shall not need you, said the hermit and all his fellows, it is but heaviness of your blood, ye shall be well mended by the grace of God tomorn. My fair lords, said Sir Launcelot, wit you well my careful body will into the earth, I have warning more than now I will say; therefore give me my rites. So when he was houseled and enelid, and had all that a Christian man ought to have, he prayed the Bishop that his fellows might bear his body to Joyous Gard. ...

And on the morn the Bishop did his mass of requiem; and after, the Bishop and all the nine knights put Sir Launcelot in the same horse bier that Queen Guenever was laid in tofore that she was buried. And so the Bishop and they all together went with the body of Sir Launcelot daily, till they came to Joyous

Gard; and ever they had an hundred torches burning about him.
And so within fifteen days they came to Joyous Gard. And there
they laid his corpse in the body of the quire, and sang and read
many psalters and prayers over him and about him. And ever his
visage was laid open and naked, that all folks might behold him.
For such was the custom in those days, that all men of worship
should so lie with open visage till that they were buried. . . .

Thus they kept Sir Launcelot's corpse on loft fifteen days, and
then they buried it with great devotion.

Sir Thomas Malory (d. 1471), *Le Morte D'Arthur*, Book XXI, chapter 12.

Love's particle returning to its source

War and Peace opens with Prince Andrey an admirer of Napoleon, but his
experiences of war (he is severely wounded at Austerlitz) and his failed
attempts at the social improvement of his own estate leave him profoundly
sceptical. Though he is unconvinced by the religiously based idealism of his
friend Pierre, discussions with Pierre provoke further reflection, as does his
own love for Natasha, to whom he becomes engaged, and by whom he is
nursed after being mortally wounded at the battle of Borodino. Though the
translation speaks of 'extreme unction', this is misleading, as Orthodoxy
uses anointing much more widely than the Western tradition – even
sometimes as a form of preparation for communion for the healthy. In any
case, Tolstoy's primary focus lies not there, but in the presentation of death
as the return of 'a particle of love' to its source.

In the past Prince Andrey had dreaded the end. Twice he had
experienced that terribly agonising feeling of the dread of death,
of the end, and now he had ceased to understand it.

The first time he had experienced that feeling when the
grenade was rotating before him, and he looked at the stubble, at
the bushes, at the sky, and knew that death was facing him.
When he had come to himself after his wound, and instantly, as
though set free from the cramping bondage of life, there had
sprung up in his soul that flower of love, eternal, free, not
dependent on this life, he had no more fear, and no more
thought, of death.

In those hours of solitary suffering and half-delirium that he
spent afterwards, the more he passed in thought into that new
element of eternal love, revealed to him, the further he uncon-
sciously travelled from earthly life. To love everything, every one,
to sacrifice self always for love, meant to love no one, meant not
to live this earthly life. And the further he penetrated into that

element of love, the more he renounced life, and the more completely he annihilated that fearful barrier that love sets up between life and death. . . .

As he fell asleep he was still thinking of what he had been thinking about all the time – of life and of death. And most of death. He felt he was closer to it.

'Love? What is love?' he thought.

'Love hinders death. Love is life. All, all that I understand, I understand only because I love. All is, all exists only because I love. All is bound up in love alone. Love is God, and dying means for me, a particle of love, to go back to the universal and eternal source of love.' These thoughts seemed to him comforting. But they were only thoughts. Something was wanting in them; there was something one-sided and personal, something intellectual; they were not self-evident. And there was uneasiness, too, and obscurity. He fell asleep.

He dreamed that he was lying in the very room in which he was lying in reality, but that he was not ill, but quite well. Many people of various sorts, indifferent people of no importance, were present. He was talking and disputing with them about some trivial matter. They seemed to be preparing to set off somewhere. Prince Andrey had a dim feeling that all this was of no consequence, and that he had other matters of graver moment to think of, but still he went on uttering empty witticisms of some sort that surprised them. By degrees all these people began to disappear, and the one thing left was the question of closing the door. He got up and went towards the door to close it and bolt it. *Everything* depended on whether he were in time to shut it or not. He was going, he was hurrying, but his legs would not move, and he knew that he would not have time to shut the door, but still he was painfully straining every effort to do so. And an agonising terror came upon him. And that terror was the fear of death; behind the door stood *It*. But while he is helplessly and clumsily struggling towards the door, that something awful is already pressing against the other side of it, and forcing the door open. Something not human – death – is forcing the door open, and he must hold it to. He clutches at the door with a last straining effort – to shut it is impossible, at least to hold it – but his efforts are feeble and awkward; and, under the pressure of that awful thing, the door opens and shuts again.

Once more *It* was pressing on the door from without. His last, supernatural efforts are vain, and both leaves of the door are noiselessly opened. *It* comes in, and it is *death*. And Prince Andrey died.

But at the instant when in his dream he died, Prince Andrey recollected that he was asleep; and at the instant when he was dying, he made an effort and waked up.

'Yes, that was death. I died and I waked up. Yes, death is an awakening,' flashed with sudden light into his soul, and the veil that had till then hidden the unknown was lifted before his spiritual vision. He felt, as it were, set free from some force that held him in bondage, and was aware of that strange lightness of being that had not left him since. ...

His last days and hours passed in a simple and commonplace way. Princess Marya and Natasha, who never left his side, both felt that. They did not weep nor shudder, and towards the last they both felt they were waiting not on him (he was no more; he had gone far away from them), but on the nearest memory of him – his body. The feelings of both of them were so strong that the external, horrible side of death did not affect them, and they did not find it needful to work up their grief. They did not weep either in his presence nor away from him, and they never even talked of him together. They felt that they could not express in words what they understood.

They both saw that he was slowly and quietly slipping further and further away from them, and both knew that this must be so, and that it was well. He received absolution and extreme unction; every one came to bid him good-bye. When his son was brought in to him, he pressed his lips to him and turned away, not because it was painful or sad to him (Princess Marya and Natasha saw that), but simply because he supposed he had done all that was required of him. But he was told to give him his blessing, he did what was required, and looked round as though to ask whether there was anything else he must do. When the body, deserted by the spirit, passed through its last struggles, Princess Marya and Natasha were there.

'It is over!' said Princess Marya, after the body had lain for some moments motionless, and growing cold before them. Natasha went close, glanced at the dead eyes, and made haste to shut them. She closed them, and did not kiss them, but hung over what was the nearest memory of him. 'Where has he gone? Where is he now?'

Leo Tolstoy (1828–1910), *War and Peace*, Part 12, chapter 16, translated by Constance Garnett.

What the waves whispered

'I hear and behold God in every object', Whitman wrote, adding 'yet understand not God in the least'. Accepting that, despite all forms of revelation, the divine remains ultimately a mystery, Whitman had, nevertheless, a pervasive sense of the sacramental: 'I see something of God each hour of the twenty-four, and each moment then, / In the faces of men and women I see God ... / I find letters from God dropt in the street, and every one is signed by God's name' (*Song of Myself*). 'Out of the Cradle' is about death understood by recalling a mystical experience of childhood. Unlike Tolstoy, for whom Love names feelings of release into the divine, Whitman contrasts love, which binds us painfully to the world, with a comfort which finally lies deeper than all pain. The vehicles of Whitman's knowledge of the divine mystery are a bird (the 'singer solitary'), whose 'cries of unsatisfied love' for its dead mate are a revelation of irremediable loss; and the sea, an intimation of quite opposite feelings.

> O you singer solitary, singing by yourself, projecting me,
> O solitary me listening, never more shall I cease perpetuating
>   you,
> Never more shall I escape, never more the reverberations,
> Never more the cries of unsatisfied love be absent from me,
> Never again leave me to be the peaceful child I was before
>   what there in the night,
> By the sea under the yellow and sagging moon,
> The messenger there arous'd, the fire, the sweet hell within,
> The unknown want, the destiny of me.
>
> O give me the clew! (it lurks in the night here somewhere,)
> O if I am to have so much, let me have more!
>
> A word then, (for I will conquer it,)
> The word final, superior to all,
> Subtle, sent up – what is it? – I listen;
> Are you whispering it, and have been all the time, you sea-
>   waves?
> Is that it from your liquid rims and wet sands?
>
> Whereto answering, the sea,
> Delaying not, hurrying not,
> Whisper'd me through the night, and very plainly before day-
>   break,
> Lisp'd to me the low and delicious word death,
> And again death, death, death, death,
> Hissing melodious, neither like the bird nor like my arous'd
>   child's heart,

But edging near as privately for me rustling at my feet,
Creeping thence steadily up to my ears and laving me softly
      all over,
Death, death, death, death, death.

Which I do not forget,
But fuse the song of my dusky demon and brother,
That he sang to me in the moonlight on Paumanok's gray
      beach,
With the thousand responsive songs at random,
My own songs awaked from that hour,
And with them the key, the word up from the waves,
The word of the sweetest song and all songs,
That strong and delicious word which, creeping to my feet,
(Or like some old crone rocking the cradle, swathed in sweet
      garments, bending aside,)
The sea whisper'd me.

          Walt Whitman (1819–91), from 'Out of the Cradle'.

With lamp well trimmed

The Reformation objected to extreme unction for a number of reasons, including lack of biblical precedent and the key role given to the priest. But perhaps chief among them was the conviction that the possibility it afforded of last-minute repentance not only effectively undermined the seriousness with which the rest of life was viewed, but encouraged repentance for the wrong reasons. Such worries are well illustrated by the earlier extract from Greene's *Brighton Rock*, with Pinkie happily contemplating murder and some far distant repentance. The High Churchman, Jeremy Taylor, chaplain to Archbishop Laud and Charles I, and author of the spiritual classics *Holy Living* and *Holy Dying*, shared these objections, though he is careful to qualify his view by observing the appropriateness of the sacrament when administered as the proper culmination of a Christian life. His argument is illustrated by reference to Christ's parable of the wise and foolish virgins with their lamps (Matt 25:1–13).

    I know no other great difference in the visitation and treating of sick persons, than what depends upon the article of late repentance; for all Churches agree in the same essential propositions, and assist the sick by the same internal ministries; as for *external*, I mean *unction*, used in the Church of Rome, since it is used when the man is above half dead, when he can exercise no act of understanding, it must needs be nothing; for no rational man can think that any ceremony can make a spiritual change without a spiritual act of him that is to be changed; nor work by way of nature, or by charm; but morally and after the manner of reasonable creatures; and therefore I do not think that ministry at all fit to be reckoned among the advantages of sick persons. . . .

The sick man's exercise of grace formerly acquired, his perfecting repentance begun in the days of health, the prayers and counsels of the holy man that ministers, the giving the Holy Sacrament, the ministry and assistance of Angels, and the mercies of God, the peace of conscience and the peace of the Church are all the assistance and preparatives that can help to dress his lamp. But if a man shall go to buy oil, when the Bridegroom comes, if his lamp be not first furnished, and then trimmed, *that* in his life, *this* upon his death-bed, his station shall be without doors, his portion with unbelievers, and the unction of the dying man shall no more strengthen his soul, than it cures his body, and the prayers for him after his death shall be of the same force as if they should pray that he should return to life again the next day, and live as long as *Lazarus* in his return. But I consider, that it is not well, that men should pretend anything will do a man good when he dies, and yet the same ministries and ten times more assistances are found for forty or fifty years together to be ineffectual. Can extreme unction at last cure what the Holy Sacrament of the Eucharist all his lifetime could not do? Can prayers for a dead man do him more good than when he was alive? If *all his days* the man belonged to death and the dominion of sin, and from thence could not be recovered by sermons, and counsels, and perpetual precepts, and frequent sacraments, by confessions and absolutions, by prayers and advocations, by external ministries and internal acts, it is but too certain that his lamp cannot then be furnished. His extreme unction is only then of use when it is made by the oil that burned in his lamp in all the days of his expectation and waiting for the coming of the Bridegroom.

Jeremy Taylor (1613–67), Epistle Dedicatory to Holy Dying.

A sigh and a sign

Just such a last-minute repentance is provided by Evelyn Waugh, though arguably this case lacks any of the features which make Pinkie's attitude so objectionable. The narrator of *Brideshead Revisited*, Charles Ryder, is an agnostic friend of Sebastian and in love with Julia, two of the children of the old Roman Catholic family, the Marchmains. Lord Marchmain had deserted the family to live in Venice with his mistress, and only returns to the ancestral seat at Brideshead – still without faith – upon the death of his wife. The scene below describes his death-bed recovery of faith as the priest utters the formula of absolution (*ego te absolvo*) and anoints him with oil. Waugh clearly intends to indicate the recovery of a religious sensibility which Marchmain had lost: as with the tearing of the Temple curtain (Mark 15:38), a new order has begun.

The priest bent over Lord Marchmain and blessed him. Julia and Cara knelt at the foot of the bed. The doctor, the nurse, and I stood behind them.

'Now,' said the priest, 'I know you are sorry for all the sins of your life, aren't you? Make a sign, if you can. You're sorry, aren't you?' But there was no sign. 'Try and remember your sins; tell God you are sorry. I am going to give you absolution. While I am giving it, tell God you are sorry you have offended him.' He began to speak in Latin. I recognized the words '*ego te absolvo in nomine Patris* ...' and saw the priest make the sign of the cross. Then I knelt, too, and prayed: 'O God, if there is a God, forgive him his sins, if there is such a thing as sin,' and the man on the bed opened his eyes and gave a sigh, the sort of sigh I had imagined people made at the moment of death, but his eyes moved so that we knew there was still life in him.

I suddenly felt the longing for a sign, if only of courtesy, if only for the sake of the woman I loved, who knelt in front of me, praying, I knew, for a sign. It seemed so small a thing that was asked, the bare acknowledgement of a present, a nod in the crowd. I prayed more simply; 'God forgive him his sins' and 'Please God, make him accept your forgiveness.'

So small a thing to ask.

The priest took the little silver box from his pocket and spoke again in Latin, touching the dying man with an oil wad; he finished what he had to do, put away the box and gave the final blessing. Suddenly Lord Marchmain moved his hand to his forehead; I thought he had felt the touch of the chrism and was wiping it away. 'O God,' I prayed, 'don't let him do that.' But there was no need for fear; the hand moved slowly down his breast, then to his shoulder, and Lord Marchmain made the sign of the cross. Then I knew that the sign I had asked for was not a little thing, not a passing nod of recognition, and a phrase came back to me from my childhood of the veil of the temple being rent from top to bottom.

Evelyn Waugh (1903–66), *Brideshead Revisited*, Book 3, chapter 5.

The threshold of eternal night

That our past can sometimes exercise too strong an influence upon us and so preclude last-minute repentance is suggested by the story of *Madame Bovary*. When first published in 1857, the novel was prosecuted because of its sympathetic portrayal of adultery. But despite several attempts to find an ideal of love outside marriage, the story ends with Emma Bovary swallowing arsenic, because all these attempts have ended in failure and she is now also desperately in debt. Educated in a convent and at times intensely religious, she receives the last rites from the Abbé Bournisien, to whom she had turned (unsuccessfully) once before for help, when first tempted towards adultery. But, though there is a powerful evocation of the form of the rite, Emma dies in despair, the song she hears reminding her of one of her lovers. Flaubert seems to blame the Church as much as Madame Bovary herself. Mere form, however beautifully effected, is not enough.

> Slowly she turned her head, and, of a sudden, as her eyes lighted on the violet stole, an expression of joy irradiated her countenance. A strange peace descended upon her, and she doubtless experienced, yet again, those mystical exaltations she had known as a child, and glimpsed the glories of the world to come.
>
> The priest rose from his knees to take the crucifix; and then she stretched forth her neck like one athirst and, gluing her lips to the body of the Man-God, she fastened thereon, with all her failing strength, the most passionate kiss of love she had ever in her life bestowed. Then he recited the *Misereatur* and the *Indulgentiam*, dipped his right thumb in the oil, and began the unctions, anointing her, first on the eyes which had gazed so covetously on the luxuries of the world; then, on the nostrils that had delighted in the breeze's soft caress and in all love-laden perfumes; then, on the mouth, the gateway of her lies, that had moaned in the moments of triumphant passion and cried aloud in the delirium of the senses; then, on the hands which had loved all things gentle to the touch; and, lastly, on the soles of the feet that, aforetime, had sped so swiftly to the appeasement of her desires, and now would stir no more.
>
> The *curé* wiped his fingers, and threw the wads of cotton-wool into the fire. Then he came back and sat by the bedside of the dying woman, warning her that it now behoved her to unite her sufferings with Christ's and surrender herself to the divine mercy.
>
> At the conclusion of his exhortations, he tried to put a consecrated taper in her hands as a symbol of the heavenly

glories which would soon encompass her. Emma had not strength enough in her fingers to hold it, and had not Monsieur Bournisien been at hand to catch it, the taper would have fallen to the floor.

However, she was not so pale now, and her countenance had assumed an expression of serenity, as though the Sacrament had made her whole again. . . .

Suddenly there was a noise of heavy clogs on the pavement outside and the scraping of a stick, and a voice, a raucous voice, began to sing,

> *Now skies are bright, the summer's here,*
> *A maiden thinks upon her dear.*

Emma sat bolt upright like a corpse suddenly galvanised into life, her hair dishevelled, her eyes fixed in a glassy stare, gaping with horror.

> *And to gather up with care*
> *What the weary reaper leaves,*
> *My Nanette goes gleaning there,*
> *Down among the golden sheaves.*

'The blind man!' she cried, and broke out into a laugh – a ghastly, frantic, despairing laugh – thinking she saw the hideous features of the wretched being, rising up to strike terror to her soul, on the very threshold of eternal night.

> *She stooped low, the wind blew high,*
> *What a sight for mortal eye!*

She fell back in a paroxysm on to the mattress. They hurried to her side. Emma was no more.

Gustave Flaubert (1821–80), *Madame Bovary*, Part 3, chapter 8, translated by J. Lewis May.

Sealed eyes see

Dowson's short but real life was quite as unhappy as Emma Bovary's fictitious one. He fell in love with a twelve-year-old girl and a few years later both his parents committed suicide within months of each other. Yet this poem captures well the optimism of unction as each of the senses is anointed for its transformation. The anointing precedes the final reception of the eucharist, known as the 'viaticum', the 'provision for the journey' to the next life. In contrast to Hopkins' concern with this life (Randal's move from strength to weakness and from cursing to a 'heavenlier heart'), for Dowson what matters is a transformation that continues beyond the grave.

> Upon the eyes, the lips, the feet,
>   On all the passages of sense,
> The atoning oil is spread with sweet
>   Renewal of lost innocence.
>
> The feet, that lately ran so fast
>   To meet desire, are soothly sealed;
> The eyes, that were so often cast
>   On vanity, are touched and healed.
>
> From troublous sights and sounds set free;
>   In such a twilight hour of breath,
> Shall one retrace his life, or see,
>   Through shadows, the true face of death?
>
> Vials of mercy! Sacring oils!
>   I know not where nor when I come,
> Nor through what wanderings and toils,
>   To crave of you Viaticum.
>
> Yet, when the walls of flesh grow weak,
>   In such an hour, it well may be,
> Through mist and darkness, light will break,
>   And each anointed sense will see.
>
>   Ernest Dowson (1867–1900), 'Extreme Unction'.

Bones with beauty clad

But what form will the transformation of which Dowson speaks take? Though Christians have sometimes conceived the afterlife in purely spiritual terms, the affirmation in the Apostles' Creed of 'the resurrection of the body' suggests otherwise, even if, as Paul observes (1 Cor 15:35–50), the new body will be as different as a plant is from the seed from which it grew. Because in some translations the phrase 'spiritual body' is used, Paul has often been misinterpreted as wishing to deny the relevance of our physical bodies: like Herbert in this poem, his real concern was to assert the sacramental transformation of both body and soul in and through death – 'Souls shall wear their new array', and 'all thy bones with beauty shall be clad', as Herbert writes. The matter through which God has acted in life will reach its appropriate fulfilment in death, however different its form might be.

Death, thou wast once an uncouth hideous thing,
    Nothing but bones,
      The sad effect of sadder groans:
Thy mouth was open, but thou couldst not sing.

For we considered thee as at some six
    Or ten years hence,
      After the loss of life and sense,
Flesh being turned to dust, and bones to sticks.

We looked on this side of thee, shooting short;
    Where we did find
      The shells of fledge souls left behind,
Dry dust, which sheds no tears, but may extort.

But since our Saviour's death did put some blood
    Into thy face,
      Thou art grown fair and full of grace,
Much in request, much sought for, as a good;

For we do now behold thee gay and glad,
    As at doomsday,
      When souls shall wear their new array,
And all thy bones with beauty shall be clad.

Therefore we can go die as sleep, and trust
    Half that we have
      Unto an honest faithful grave,
Making our pillows either down, or dust.

    George Herbert (1593–1633), 'Death' from *The Temple*.

The blossoming graves

By the time Kilvert's *Diary* was discovered in 1938, most of it had already been destroyed by relatives. What remains records ten years of his ministry in the Welsh border country before his early death from peritonitis. His obvious sympathy with nature is here combined with a recurring Christian theme regarding its sacramental significance: that new life through death in nature mirrors the resurrection. Certainly, the Church Fathers were in no doubt about the appropriateness of Easter coinciding with spring, while in English, according to Bede, the very term is derived from the name of an Anglo-Saxon spring goddess (Eostre). As Kilvert observes, while the church inside is decorated for Easter as the day of new life, outside the very graves look as though they are being prepared for the general resurrection. Such concordance between nature and Christian doctrine is beautifully expressed in lines by one of his contemporaries, Christina Rossetti: 'Lord, purge our eyes to see / Within the seed a tree, / Within the glowing egg a bird, / Within the shroud a butterfly; / Till, taught by such we see, / Beyond all creatures, Thee.'

I awoke at 4.30 and there was a glorious sight in the sky, one of the grand spectacles of the Universe. There was not a cloud in the deep wonderful blue of the heavens. Along the Eastern horizon there was a clear deep intense glow neither scarlet nor crimson but a mixture of both. This red glow was very narrow, almost like a riband and it suddenly shaded off into the deep blue. Opposite in the west the full moon shining in all its brilliance was setting upon the hill beyond the church steeple. Thus the glow in the east bathed the church in a warm rich tinted light, while the moon from the west was casting strong shadows. The moon dropped quickly down behind the hill bright to the last, till only her rim could be seen sparkling among the tops of the orchards on the hill. The sun rose quickly and his rays struck red upon the white walls of Penllan, but not so brilliantly as in the winter sunrisings. I got up soon after 5 and set to work on my Easter sermon getting two hours for writing before breakfast.

At 11 I went to the school. Next I went to Cae Mawr. Mrs Morrell had been very busy all the morning preparing decorations for the Font, a round dish full of flowers in water and just big enough to fit into the Font and upon this large dish a pot filled and covered with flowers all wild, primroses, violets, wood anemones, wood sorrel, periwinkles, oxlips and the first blue bells, rising in a gentle pyramid, ferns and larch sprays drooping over the brim, a wreath of simple ivy to go round the stem of the Font, and a bed of moss to encircle the foot of the Font in a narrow band pointed at the corners and angles of the stone with knots of primroses. At 2 o'clock Hetty Gore of the Holly House came down from Cefn y Blaen and upset all my arrangements for the afternoon saying that old William Pritchard there was very ill, not likely to live, and wishes to see me this afternoon that I might read to him and give him the Sacrament. Hetty Gore thought he might not last many days. So I was obliged to go to the Vicarage, explain, and give up my drive. Found the schoolmaster and a friend staying with him just going out to get moss and carrying the East window-sill board from the Church to the school to prepare it for tomorrow with the text 'Christ is Risen' written in primroses upon moss. Shall I ever forget that journey up the hill to Cefn y Blaen in this burning Easter Eve, under the cloudless blue, the scorching sun and over the country covered with a hot dim haze? I climbed up the Bron panting in the sultry afternoon heat. Went up the fields from Court Evan Gwynne to Little Wern y Pentre and envied the sheep that were being washed in the brook below, between the field and the lane, by Price of Great Wern y Pentre and his excited boys. The peewits were sweeping rolling and tumbling in the hot blue air about the Tall Trees with a strange deep mysterious hustling and quavering sound from their great wings. . . .

When I started for Cefn y Blaen only two or three people were in the churchyard with flowers. But now the customary beautiful Easter Eve Idyll had fairly begun and people kept arriving from all parts with flowers to dress the graves. Children were coming from the town and from neighbouring villages with baskets of flowers and knives to cut holes in the turf. The roads were lively with people coming and going and the churchyard a busy scene with women and children and a few men moving about among the tombstones and kneeling down beside the green mounds flowering the graves. . . .

More and more people kept coming into the churchyard as they finished their day's work. The sun went down in glory behind the dingle, but still the work of love went on through the twilight and into the dusk until the moon rose full and splendid. The figures continued to move about among the graves and to bend over the green mounds in the calm clear moonlight and warm air of the balmy evening. . . .

At 8 o'clock there was a gathering of the Choir in the Church to practise the two anthems for to-morrow. The moonlight came streaming in broadly through the chancel windows. When the choir had gone and the lights were out and the church quiet again, as I walked down the Churchyard alone the decked graves had a strange effect in the moonlight and looked as if the people had laid down to sleep for the night out of doors, ready dressed to rise early on Easter morning. I lingered in the verandah before going to bed. The air was as soft and warm as a summer night, and the broad moonlight made the quiet village almost as light as day. Everyone seemed to have gone to rest and there was not a sound except the clink and trickle of the brook.

Francis Kilvert (1840–79), *Diary*, Easter Eve, 1870.

Only Thee

But is the sacramental really to continue beyond the grave? Will God continue to mediate himself through some form of matter, or is not all mediation then at an end, and we see God face to face? For some, God placed such value upon his creation in becoming incarnate within it that matter, however transformed, must continue to have its place: the vision of 'a new heaven and a new earth' of which Revelation 21 speaks is more than metaphor. But the same metaphor can be read in a quite opposite way, so that for others, like Mary Coleridge, all sacraments must have their ending when at length we pass beyond this present, material realm: nature will no more need to point beyond itself, since the true Light will have replaced all other lights (Rev 21:23).

> There, in that other world, what waits for me?
> What shall I find after that other birth?
> No stormy, tossing, foaming, smiling sea,
>   But a new earth.
>
> No sun to mark the changing of the days,
> No slow, soft falling of the alternate night,
> No moon, no star, no light upon my ways,
>   Only the Light.
>
> No gray cathedral, wide and wondrous fair,
> That I may tread where all my fathers trod.
> Nay, nay, my soul, no house of God is there,
>   But only God.
>
>   Mary Coleridge (1861–1907), 'There'.

INDEX OF AUTHORS